Impact of Modernization on Development and Demographic Behaviour

Case Studies in Seven Third World Countries

Edited by
Carol Vlassoff and Barkat-e-Khuda

Vlassoff, C.
Barkat-e-Khuda

IDRC-260e
    Impact of modernization on development and demographic behaviour : case studies in seven Third World countries. Ottawa, Ont., IDRC, 1988. xi + 123 p. : ill.

/Rural development/, /modernization/, /fertility/, /communities/, /Philippines/, /Malaysia/, /Bangladesh/, /India/, /Colombia/, /Peru/, /Argentina/ — /case studies/, /fertility determinants/, /economic behaviour/, /social implications/, /household/, /cottage industry/, /child labour/.

UDC: 312(5:8)   ISBN: 0-88936-502-4

This work was carried out with the aid of grants from the International Development Research Centre. The views expressed are those of the authors and do not necessarily represent the views of the Centre. Mention of a proprietary name does not constitute endorsement of the product and is given only for information.

CONTRIBUTORS

Barkat-e-Khuda
Department of Economics, Dhaka University, Dhaka 2, Bangladesh

Carol Vlassoff
Special Programme for Research and Training in Tropical Diseases,
World Health Organization, 1211 Geneva 27, Switzerland

Robert A. Hackenberg
Department of Anthropology, University of Colorado, Campus Box
233, Boulder, CO, 80309-0233, USA

Aihwa Ong
Department of Anthropology, University of California, Berkeley, CA
94720, USA

Amit Bhattacharyya
Population Division, Department of International Economics and
Social Affairs, United Nations, New York, NY, 10017, USA

Adrian C. Hayes
Social Sciences (340), State University of New York at Albany,
Albany, NY, 12222, USA

Diego Giraldo Samper
División de Salud, Asociación Colombiana de Facultades de Medicina,
Apartado Aéreo 53751, Bogotá, D.F., Colombia

Floreal Forni
Centro de Estudios e Investigaciones Laborales, Montevideo 666,
Capital Federal, Argentina

Roberto Benencia
Centro de Estudios e Investigaciones Laborales, Montevideo 666,
Capital Federal, Argentina

Carlos E. Aramburú
Instituto Andino de Estudios en Población y Desarrollo, Lola Pardo
Vargas (325), Urbanización Aurura, Miraflores, Lima 18, Peru

ABSTRACT

The collection of articles in this volume focuses on the impact of rural development policies and projects on demographic behaviour in seven countries in Asia and Latin America. The methodologies include both quantitative surveys and in-depth microlevel observation of rural communities. The Philippines study examines changes over time in two rural communities in Southern Mindanao influenced by the Green Revolution and agrarian reform. The Malaysian project investigates the impact of modern industrial expansion in a traditional rural area upon the family economy and gender roles. In Bangladesh, the effect of an integrated program for rural development upon demographic change, especially on fertility and family-planning behaviour, is examined. The Indian study focuses on the relationship between child labour and fertility in a village where jewelry-making is an important cottage industry. In rural Colombia, demographic and economic behaviour are compared in three different economic sectors — modern capitalist, traditional capitalist, and smallholders. The Argentinian study investigates the demographic and economic characteristics of households belonging to different agricultural sectors of a relatively underdeveloped province. Finally, in Peru, demographic and economic behaviour in four rural areas, characterized by different levels of development, are compared. The final chapter draws together common insights from the seven studies and provides general conclusions on what has been learned about the economic, demographic, and social effects of development on rural households.

RÉSUMÉ

Cette série d'articles traite des effets de politiques de développement rural et de projets sur le comportement démographique de la population dans sept pays de l'Asie et de l'Amérique latine. Les méthodologies employées comprennent notamment des études quantitatives et des études approfondies des collectivités rurales. Le projet philippin porte sur les changements qui se sont produits dans deux collectivités rurales du sud de Mindanao, touchées par la Révolution agricole et la réforme agraire. Le projet malaysien étudie, dans une région rurale traditionnelle, les effets de l'expansion industrielle moderne sur le revenu des familles et le rôle des sexes. Au Bangladesh, les chercheurs se sont penchés sur l'incidence démographique d'un programme de développement rural intégré, en particulier sur la fécondité et le comportement de la population face à la régulation des naissances. En Inde, ils ont étudié les liens entre le travail des enfants et la fécondité dans un village oué la bijouterie constitue une industrie artisanale importante. En Colombie, ils ont fait une étude comparative du comportement démographique et économique de la population rurale dans trois différents secteurs de l'économie — capitalisme moderne, capitalisme traditionel et petites exploitations agricoles. L'étude menée en Argentine s'intéresse aux charactéristiques démographiques et économiques de ménages appartenant à différents secteurs agricoles dans une province relativement sous-développée. Enfin, au Pérou, les chercheurs ont comparé le comportement démographique et économique de la population de quatre régions rurales à divers stades de développement. Le dernier chapitre fait la synthéése des idées communes aux sept études et tire des conclusions générales concernant les effets économiques, démographiques et sociaux du développement sur les familles rurales.

RESUMEN

Los artículos que conforman este volumen se centran en el impacto de las políticas y proyectos de desarrollo rural sobre el comportamiento demográfico en siete países de Asia y América Latina. Las metodologías incluyen tanto estudios cuantitativos como profundas observaciones de las comunidades rurales a nivel micro. El estudio filipino examina los cambios ocurridos en dos comunidades rurales del sur de Mindanao influidas por la revolución verde y la reforma agraria. El proyecto malasio investiga el impacto de la expansión industrial moderna en un área rural tradicional sobre la economía familiar y el papel de los sexos. En Bangladesh, se examina el efecto de un programa integrado de desarrollo rural sobre el cambio demográfico, especialmente la fecundidad y la planificación familiar. El estudio de India se centra en la relación entre trabajo infantil y fecundidad en una aldea donde la joyería es una importante industria casera. En Colombia rural se comparan los comportamientos demográfico y económico de tres sectores económicos diferentes — capitalista moderno, capitalista tradicional y pequeños agricultores. El estudio argentino investiga las características demográficas y económicas de hogares pertenecientes a diversos sectores agrícolas de una provincia relativamente subdesarrollada. Finalmente, en Perú, se comparan los comportamientos demográficos y económicos de cuatro áreas rurales caracterizadas por distintos niveles de desarrollo. El capítulo final reúne las apreciaciones de los siete estudios y ofrece conclusiones generales sobre lo que se ha aprendido acerca del los efectos económicos, demográficos y sociales del desarrollo sobre los hogares rurales.

CONTENTS

FOREWORD

Over the past decade, researchers and policymakers in Third World countries have been asking how development projects and policies, aimed primarily at economic well-being, have affected demographic behaviour. More specifically, to what extent have development programs affected the fertility, migration, and mortality patterns of families in developing countries, particularly of those in rural areas where most poor Third World families live?

Although interest in this topic is universal, approaches to the study of household demographic behaviour have varied markedly in different parts of the world. In Latin America, the concept of "survival strategies" has been widely used to explain why poor rural families have large numbers of children. Because children contribute to the family economy through their labour, both on the farm and through migration and the remittances they provide, it has been argued that a large number of children represents a rational strategy for a family's survival. In other parts of the world, including Asia and Africa, a more common approach has been an empirical or neoclassical interpretation, in which the determinants of demographic behaviour are examined from a microeconomic or individual perspective. Demographic trends in fertility and migration, for example, are viewed as individual responses to imbalances of various kinds, such as land or resources, capital or labour, rather than as a group or family strategy.

In the late 1970s, proposals from five countries — Bangladesh, Korea, Malaysia, the Philippines, and Tanzania — were selected by IDRC to undertake pioneering projects on the topic of development and demographic response. In the early 1980s, projects were also funded in five Latin American countries — Argentina, Brazil, Colombia, Mexico, and Peru.

When these projects were completed or nearing completion in 1983, a further project was supported to allow for more in-depth analysis, interpretation, and synthesis of the research findings from the separate studies. A comparative workshop was held in Vancouver, Canada, in October 1984 at which the papers contained in this volume were presented.

For various reasons, not all the papers are reproduced in this volume — some (including the Tanzanian paper) fell somewhat outside the main focus of the topic and were considered more appropriate for alternative publications; others were not satisfactorily completed or revised. This volume, therefore, represents only a selection of the wide range of findings on this important topic. Nonetheless, through the insights of microstudies and survey data from both Asia and Latin America, it makes a significant contribution to a broader understanding of the impact of development activities on rural Third World families.

Anne V. Whyte

Director, Social Sciences Division
International Development Research Centre

ACKNOWLEDGMENTS

Several important players were involved in organizing and assisting the various teams, and their contributions are gratefully acknowledged. They include Dr Moni Nag (Population Council), who attended project workshops and provided valuable input; Dr Alan B. Simmons (Director, Centre for Research on Latin America and the Caribbean), who initiated many of the projects and conceptualized several of their activities; Ms Shirley B. Seward (Director, Institute for Research on Public Policy), who played a key role in the inception of the Asian and African network; and Ms Nicole Beaudoin-Dutcher (Conference Coordinator, Canadian College of Health Service Executives), who organized the Vancouver meeting and typed the first drafts of many of the chapters of this volume. Special thanks are also accorded to Dr Mario Torres (IDRC) for his help with the Latin American studies and, last but not least, to Ms Constance Gagnon (IDRC) who has patiently and cheerfully typed successive versions of the manuscript and assisted with the final organizational and financial aspects of the projects.

We also acknowledge the authors of those studies that formed part of the Vancouver meeting but are not included here for their advice and general support in contributing to the papers in the volume. They are Dr Luis Lenero (Director, Instituto Mexicano de Estudios Sociales), who also acted as a coordinator for the Latin American studies and advised the various teams on their research; Drs Vilmar Faria and Elza Berquó (Centro Brasileiro de Análise e Planejamento); and Drs Mo-im Kim and Byung-Joon Ahn (Yonsei University). The Korean project was hampered by the departure of Dr Mo-im Kim to an official government position and Dr Ahn and his team must be congratulated for finishing the study according to its original objectives.

INTRODUCTION

Barkat-e-Khuda and Carol Vlassoff

Third World countries, which account for a dominant share of the world's population, are diverse in size, culture, religion, political systems, and levels of socioeconomic development. Although rapid economic development has taken place over the past several decades in some Third World countries, many others remain largely untouched by this process: the majority of the population remains illiterate and lives in abject poverty, especially in the rural areas. The overwhelming size of the rural population, its agrarian base and reliance on massive food aid, and the fact that so much of it lives below or at the poverty line, make it essential that development efforts be focused on the rural poor.

Governments in many Third World countries are aware of their problems, and have taken various measures to improve living conditions. In many of these nations, for example, technological progress has been made in developing high-yielding varieties of paddy and wheat. Schemes for rural industrialization have been adopted by some countries to provide employment for women and to ensure employment for men during the lean agricultural season, thereby improving levels of income. Agrarian reform has also been implemented in many countries to provide a more equitable distribution of land among the peasantry. Schemes to reduce population pressure in the densely settled areas have also been set up in some countries; these include creating economic incentives for people to relocate to less populated areas.

It is generally agreed that economic development can be affected either positively or negatively by demographic changes. On the other hand, development projects may also have demographic consequences. By raising rural incomes, rural development projects may cause fertility to decline. This happens when, for instance, as a result of higher incomes, parents are able to afford schooling for their children: thus, costs incurred for children rise and parents are motivated to limit their fertility. Schooling delays marriage among educated youth, and increased age at marriage generally reduces fertility. Higher incomes give families access to health facilities and, hence, to a higher level of nutrition and well-being. This, in sum, may depress infant and child mortality, which may also lead to a decline of fertility.

As a result of higher incomes and improvements in living conditions, people also change their outlook: they tend to develop perceptions of a better

1

future for themselves and their children. The new aspirations generally include the desire to improve living standards, which often competes with the desire for children.

By raising incomes, however, such development activities may also cause fertility to rise. This happens when, because nutrition and health are improved, miscarriage and infant mortality are reduced, or when, because more women are entering the labour force, periods of breastfeeding are shortened. The net demographic impact of such development inputs will thus depend on the net balance between the various kinds of demographic responses that such activities can generate.

In this volume, the demographic effects of development policies and projects in rural societies in the Third World are examined using evidence from studies in several countries in Asia and Latin America. Unlike several other recent publications on the impact of development projects on demographic behaviour, the present selections are concerned more with the combined effects of a range of development activities, of which a particular development program is often only a part. Because a diffuse array of development inputs and other changes are described, the specific effects of particular programs cannot be determined easily. Specific policy implications are, likewise, not always evident. However, the studies do take us far along in understanding broad development processes and their diverse effects on economic classes, communities, and families at the microlevel in the selected study areas.

The projects described in this book result from two networks of research teams, one from Asia and Africa, the other from Latin America, whose research was funded by the International Development Research Centre (IDRC).[1] The broad objective of the studies was to select a development project or policy, or microareas where significant development was evident, and to examine its impact upon household demographic behaviour, particularly in rural areas. Hence, the studies were not intended to be broadly representative of the countries from which they were drawn, but rather case studies of development and demographic change. Several studies, e.g., Bangladesh, Malaysia, and the Philippines, describe events and outcomes that appear to be very different from the national contexts or from events occurring elsewhere in the selected countries. Thus, they capture only a part of the complexity and variety of demographic responses to development. The methodology was to include both quantitative surveys and microlevel observation of the study areas and so provide as complete an understanding as possible of the processes involved.

The Asian–African projects were the first to get underway, and included studies from the Philippines, Malaysia, Bangladesh, India, and Korea. The Philippines study, conducted by Robert A. Hackenberg, examined changes at the household level in Southern Mindanao where substantial interregional differences in economic development were evident. In Malaysia, Aihwa Ong studied the changes experienced by rural families, and young

---

[1] *Only one of the studies, that of Bhattacharyya in India, was not funded by IDRC. However, IDRC provided support for international travel for Bhattacharyya to attend several of the project workshops.*

2

women in particular, as a result of industrial expansion into traditional rural areas. Barkat-e-Khuda examined the demographic impact of a rural development program in Comilla District, Bangladesh, especially with respect to changes in fertility behaviour. Amit Bhattacharyya investigated the effect of child labour in a cottage industry in rural West Bengal on parents' perceptions of the value of children and related fertility decisions. In Korea, Mo-im Kim and Byung-Joon Ahn compared two rural areas, one of which had been involved in the New Village Movement, the other of which had not (this study is not included here).

Only one study was supported on this topic in Africa, that by Dr Kamuzora in Tanzania (this study is not included here). The failure to have more representation from Africa was partly due to the lack of proposals from that continent, as well as the fact that fewer IDRC resources were allocated to the promotion of research on this general topic in Africa than in the other two regions.

A similar process took place in Latin America, although the focus was more on the effects of various national development initiatives than on the development projects themselves. In rural Colombia, for example, Diego Giraldo Samper undertook a study of the relationships between productive organization, family structure, and demographic behaviour in three different sectors of the economy, ranging from the modern capitalist to the traditional smallholders. Similarly, Floreal Forni and Robert Benencia compared household demographic behaviour in different agricultural sectors in irrigated and dry areas of an economically underdeveloped province of Argentina. In Peru, Carlos Aramburú compared two more-developed regions with two less-developed ones, focusing on the interaction between "external" regional factors and "internal" familial responses. Two studies were undertaken in Brazil, one by Lea Melo da Silva on fertility declines among women in the slum areas of Belo Horizonte, the other by Vilmar Faria and Elza Berquo on demographic and economic behaviour in selected regions of Brazil, focusing upon migration. Finally, Luis Lenero investigated family strategies in a rapidly developing oil-producing region of Mexico. (The studies in Brazil and Mexico are not included in this volume.)

Three workshops were held in each region during the course of these projects to allow the teams to share their experiences and to benefit from the comments and suggestions of their colleagues. When all the projects had been completed, a global meeting was held in Vancouver, Canada, in October 1984 to which the principal researchers from all the projects were invited. Although several of the researchers were unable to attend, the experience was extremely valuable for the participants and provided them with the opportunity to share their research with others interested in similar issues in different parts of the world.

This publication is a direct result of the papers presented at the Vancouver meeting. The papers were discussed by the participants and revised on the basis of the discussion with a view to publication by IDRC. As with most publications of this type, involving the contributions of many authors, it has been slower coming to fruition than was at first expected. Also, all the studies that were part of the original networks are not included here.

In some cases, the authors chose to publish their studies in full as larger manuscripts or to submit them for publication elsewhere; in others, final papers were not prepared in time to meet publication deadlines. Also, two of the studies are included in summary form only because their results were less clearly related to the topic of the demographic impact of development activities than those papers included in full. Because they do provide some interesting insights, however, summaries of these two studies are provided.

PART 1

DEMOGRAPHIC RESPONSES TO DEVELOPMENT IN ASIA AND LATIN AMERICA

UPENDING MALTHUS: THE HOUSEHOLD ROLE IN PHILIPPINE FOOD GAINS AND FERTILITY LOSSES, 1970–1980

Robert A. Hackenberg

INTRODUCTION: ESCAPING THE "POSITIVE CHECKS"

Two decades ago, it was commonplace to affirm that the Malthusian prediction of a disastrous shortfall between exploding population and stagnating agricultural growth was inevitable. It was set forth amidst myriad projections presented in 1967 by President Johnson's Science Advisory Committee, the authors of *The World Food Problem* (PSAC 1967). The predicted disaster was averted. Two decades later, we have accomplished what then seemed impossible: fertility rates have declined throughout Asia and Latin America, substantially reducing earlier projections, and we are now assured that growth of food production will continue to exceed that of population for the balance of this century (GPO 1980).

It is now clear that the evidence of the past 25 years of development has upended Malthus by scientific advances that he could not foresee. His forecast that food production could only be increased by additional land did not anticipate the Green Revolution, which achieved gains by increasing yields rather than area. In the realm of contraception, which he held to be ineffective in limiting population, new technology and distribution methods once again proved him wrong.

This paper reports data from the Philippines representing population growth and food production at two points in time, 1970 and 1980. The intervening decade, here as elsewhere, proved to be a crucial one for reversing trends in both dimensions. This study may be interpreted as a trend analysis at the micro level of the mechanisms that operated to upend Malthus in two representative rural municipalities of the Mindanao province of Davao del Sur. The discussion identifies two sources for the dramatic changes taking place. First, resident households responded to the economic forces at work in a rapidly evolving frontier environment. Second, newly established government programs provided massive political intervention.

THE SOUTHERN PHILIPPINE REGION: DEMOGRAPHIC AND ECONOMIC BACKGROUND

During the 1950s, the last decade before the closing of the frontier to further migration, more than two million migrants occupied homestead tracts in Mindanao. These migrants were examples of the traditional Philippine method for coping with a population explosion, which had reached 3.5% per year, and were bringing vast tracts of new land into cultivation.

After 1960, this cheap solution became inoperative and further gains in agricultural output were achieved by yield increases (Ruttan 1978:374). By the mid-1970s, 64% of Philippine rice fields were planted with high-yielding varieties (Hayami and Kikuchi 1981:44). Rice production increased from 1.1 to 2.0 t/ha in the two decades after 1960 (ILO 1974:442; IBRD 1980:81). Total production was assisted by an increase in irrigable land from 739 to 1607 thousand ha in the same period (Hayami and Kikuchi 1978:331–332). After decades of deficits, the Philippines attained rice self-sufficiency in 1975. However, the residual issue of population growth, which continued at 2.5% per year, remained. From 1970 to 1979, 59.3% of the expansion in the labour force was added to agriculture (USAID 1981:10).

Household economic reorganization resulted from the closing of the settlement frontier and the shift to yield-increasing technology. The peasant mode of production was no longer adaptive; it was replaced by the "new farm system." In addition to irrigation, the system required five major inputs: fertilizer, agricultural chemicals, additional labour beyond that of household members, farm machinery, and credit to finance all of them (Barker and Cordova 1978; Duff 1978; Wickham et al. 1978). Taken together, these changes amounted to commercializing production by the farm household.

These innovations, combined with persistent population growth, contain the threat of impoverishment for the rural household. The promise of increased yields tends to drive up land prices while other costs are rising. The new technology favours economies of scale. These forces may converge to drive out smallholders at the same time that population gains are driving down the price of labour. The result would be a two-class system of large landowners superimposed upon an impoverished proletariat (J.C. Scott 1976:209–210). Hayami and Kikuchi (1981:60) refer to this process as "polarization."

Polarization seems more probable in older heartland areas of Southeast Asian agriculture, such as Java or Luzon, where the plantation framework has already differentiated large operators from smallholders and tenants. On the frontiers, such as Mindanao, all are homesteaders and begin the transition to farm systems management on much the same footing. There will be competition, selection, and differentiation, but it begins from an even base. Here, Hayami and Kikuchi (1981:30) argue, increasing productivity will create more complex social organization, providing both the increments of personnel and division of functions required for farm systems operation. Responsibilities will be subdivided among a hierarchy of specialists that includes landlords, managers, share tenants, fixed-rent lessors, and finally subtenants, who are actually resident farm labourers working full time for a share of the crop. In contrast to polarization, this option is called "stratification." It shares the profits from increased crop yields much more equitably among a steadily increasing group of participants. Nonetheless, the shares paid to each class must grow smaller with the passage of time. Involution (Geertz 1963) appears to be inevitable.

There is a third option, however, which has been designated "diversification" (Hackenberg 1984a). This can evolve from a homestead pattern of land settlement. Given the Green Revolution essentials of high-yielding varieties and irrigation, it takes the form of medium-sized, owner-operated farms, linked with others to form effective producing and marketing organizations through cooperatives.

If supplemented by a conventional assortment of government policies that support agriculture — including land reform, production loans, and effective family planning — then it is reasonable to expect that descendants of farm operators will seek nonfarm employment in agricultural processing or support and service operations, at the same time as fertility reductions will restrain the accumulation of surplus farm labour that would have driven down the price of their employment.

The data presented here answer the question raised by the preceding paragraphs: can the combination of Green Revolution technology and effective family planning produce the diversification solution with its presumed combination of income growth and equitable distribution? If the answer is "yes," this combination then completely confounds the Malthusian forecast by increasing farm production at the same time as it reduces population growth rates. Further circumstances framing this alternative have been described by Hackenberg (1980, 1982, 1983).

THE DAVAO DEL SUR EXPERIMENT: A DECADE OF CHANGE, 1970–1980

Mindanao was opened for homesteading under the Public Land Law of 1903, but substantial settlement awaited the creation of a road network, which followed the Colonization Act of 1935. Simkins and Wernstedt (1971:7–9) documented the arrival of 397 000 new settlers in Davao Province between 1939 and 1960, "beyond the rate of natural increase." Of these, 118 000 went to the Digos-Padada Valley in what would become, in 1967, the province of Davao del Sur.

In 1965, the valley was effectively closed to further settlement because of depletion of land reserves. During the previous decade, its agricultural potential had been extended by construction of the 4600-ha Badagoy communal irrigation system serving 1300 farms; this was soon followed by other contiguous systems (Hackenberg 1971). The irrigated bottomlands and the adjacent rain-fed hilly slopes established two ecological regimes that separated rice lands from those planted in corn and coconut. Individual holdings

9

ranged from 1–2 ha on the valley floor to 20–30 ha on less productive upland.

The irrigated bottomlands were an ideal environment for high-yield varieties, and the first planting of "miracle rice" took place in 1967. The first Japanese hand tractors were introduced in the same year (Hackenberg 1971:22–33). Although the uplands were unsuited to become "farm systems," they received their own modernization stimuli: extensive cultivation of sugar and banana on plantation-sized holdings took place after 1965, and a sugar mill was located in the centre of the valley. Agribusiness was preceded by substantial public investment in appropriate infrastructure: highways, feeder roads, power grids, and water storage and distribution systems for expanded irrigation.

The opportunity to investigate the effect that modernization of farm households had produced through diversification was provided by two field studies of lowland (irrigated rice) and upland (corn and coconut) communities repeated after an interval of 10 years (1970 and 1980). The baseline study, supported by a contract from the United States Center for Population Research, included 2050 households divided between the municipalities of Magsaysay (valley) and Matanao (upland). Interviews covered both economic and demographic subjects and included pregnancy histories and data on all household members.

Ecological differences between the communities were paralleled by linguistic and cultural differences. Magsaysay had been settled by Ilocanos from Luzon — a thrifty, hard-working people dedicated to self-improvement. Matanao was occupied by Cebuanos from the Visayas, an area more concerned with social and religious observances than advancement. Our initial hypothesis was that, because the Ilocanos were more progressive and enjoyed an income advantage over their Cebuano neighbours, earlier fertility reductions would be evident in the lowland community.

Like most frontier areas, however, the Digos-Padada Valley was characterized by a labour shortage in the years after settlement. It was not surprising, then, that use of household labour resulted in peak fertility levels in both Magsaysay and Matanao in 1970. The young age structure of the migrant population added its own impetus to already high indigenous reproductive behaviour. If differences were to be found, the second generation (the descendants of the homesteader households) would produce them. This hypothesis was tested during the 1980 follow-up to the baseline study, funded by the International Development Research Centre (IDRC).

During the decade that elapsed between the baseline study and the 1980 follow-up, circumstances intervened that served to further differentiate upland and lowland communities. The imposition of land reform on rice and corn farmers, but not on producers of plantation crops, resulted in disposal of holdings greater than 7 ha. Because of the extensive nature of corn cultivation, this was a much greater hardship in Matanao than in Magsaysay. At the same time, the rice production loans, which became available from the national Masagana 99 credit program, increased the economic advantage of the lowland farm owner–operators.

The pattern of developmental change unfolding over the decade provided for the unexpected absorption of a substantial labour force in both communities: there was the Green Revolution in the area around Magsaysay, which demanded an additional 50% more person-days of labour input on each rice farm (Roumasset and Smith 1981) and, more important, the creation of a number of new nonfarm service and support occupations. Near Matanao, corporate farming of export crops introduced its own massive requirements for unskilled field labour.

In view of these modifications, the 1980 survey was framed by the prediction that Magsaysay, the Green Revolution rice community, would have advanced toward economic diversification with growth and equity, whereas Matanao, a corn community invaded by sugar cultivation, would be moving rapidly toward polarizing into two strata: an elite of sugar and coconut planters and a working class proletariat of farm labour. These hypotheses are examined against a selection of comparative data from the baseline study and its follow-up, after a brief description of the study design.

ANALYSIS OF SURVEY RESULTS: MAGSAYSAY AND MATANAO, 1980

The study sites are contained within the most densely settled portion of the Digos-Padada Valley, which comprises the midsection of Davao del Sur (Fig. 1). In 1970, the municipality of Magsaysay contained 18 *barrios* with a population of 30 920 and Matanao contained 32 *barrios* with a population of 26 889. In Magsaysay, the study contained the entire rice-producing area covered by the communal irrigation system, including parts of the administrative centre (*población*) and six adjacent *barrios* with a population of 6529. In Matanao, the study area circumscribed the *población* and two contiguous large *barrios* with a cross section of corn, coconut, and sugar cultivation; their population in 1970 was 5610. All study sites were mapped and all households within selected *barrios* were interviewed.

To simplify the interpretation, only the principal conclusions from the data are reviewed: a comprehensive presentation is available elsewhere (Hackenberg 1984a). Socioeconomic changes, considered as independent variables, are presented first with emphasis on the type of adaptation being pursued by each community. Next, demographic characteristics, considered as dependent variables, are evaluated.

SOCIOECONOMIC CHANGES, 1970–1980

Size of Owner-operated Farms

The most significant change over the decade was that the farm land operated by individual owners was reduced by 40%. In Magsaysay, the number of owners remained about the same but the average farm size declined from 5.96 to 3.45 ha; in Matanao, the average farm size dropped more sharply from 8.39 to 4.34 ha. The accompanying change in distribution of ownership may also be attributed to land reform. In 1970, farms

11

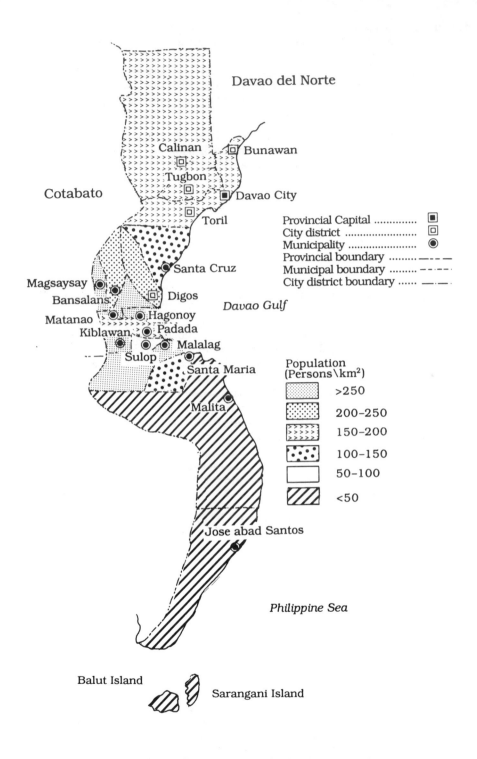

Davao del Norte

Cotabato

Calinan · ▣ Bunawan

Tugbon

■ Davao City

Toril

Santa Cruz

Magsaysay
Bansalans
Matanao · Hagonoy
Kiblawan · Padada
Sulop · Malalag
Santa Maria

Digos

Davao Gulf

Malita

Jose abad Santos

Philippine Sea

Balut Island

Sarangani Island

Provincial Capital	■
City district	▣
Municipality	◉
Provincial boundary	— — —
Municipal boundary	— - —
City district boundary	—·—·

Population
(Persons\km²)

	>250
	200–250
>>>>>	150–200
·:·:·	100–150
	50–100
⁄⁄⁄	<50

Fig. 1. Population density of Davao del Sur by municipality, 1970.

12

owned by *población* residents were 50% larger than those owned by operators residing on them. By 1980, average farm sizes in *población* and rural areas were equal.

Tenants and Leaseholders among Household Heads

At both study sites, the proportion of owners remained relatively constant (about one-third of all households); however, tenants of 1970 failed to become the leasehold operators of 1980, as land-reform planners had predicted. In Matanao, the proportion of tenants and lessors was reduced from 59.6 to 20.7%, but farm labourers among household heads increased from 8.8 to 48.7%. In Magsaysay, the lessors and tenants declined from their 1970 strength of 47.3 to 29.2% and the proportion of labourer household heads rose from 18.8 to 37.9%.

The reasons for these changes are complex but not obscure. Under Philippine land reform, an owner–operator's rice and corn lands are vulnerable only if they have been tenanted (Harkin 1975:8–9). Thus, the landlord had an incentive to remove the tenants before the fields were surveyed by the Ministry of Agrarian Reform. Kerkvliet (1974) affirms that substantial tenant removal took place in 1973 and later.

Tenants who wished to become either owners or lessors could pay a share of the crop (20–25%) to their former landlord, but had to finance all costs themselves. Since the Green Revolution, these costs had become prohibitive, making tenant/lessor status undesirable. By becoming a full-time labourer instead of a tenant, however, a household head could continue to receive a share of the crop (usually 16%) — this appeared to be a more profitable arrangement for the tenant.

Cropping Pattern

Matanao experienced the most radical change in cropping structure. In 1970, 65% of its farm operators grew corn exclusively but, by 1980, this proportion had dropped to 33%. The difference was caused by a shift to either sugar or coconut (8% each) or to a mixed cropping pattern dividing the area between a cereal (rice or corn) and a commercial crop (coconut or sugar). Mixed cropping of this sort was favoured by another 15% of former corn cultivators. The remaining 33% of Matanao's farms remained in rice cultivation (21%) or switched to new cash crops such as cacao and coffee (12%).

The pattern of Magsaysay's rice cultivation, which claimed 75% of all farms in 1970, persisted at the same level throughout the decade. Only in the *población*, where the largest landowners were found in 1970, had there been a decline in the number of rice farms (from 72.1 to 53.5%) and a complementary increase in cash crops (9.3 to 27.6%), primarily in coconut. However, the shift from corn to rice throughout the rest of the district was sufficient to compensate for this decline in the overall production of the municipality.

Income level of a farming area in 1970 was inversely related to its propensity to change its cropping pattern. In Matanao, the lowest income district in 1970 (with 90% of its farms allocated to corn) had the largest number of sugar planters among its farm operators in 1980. In Magsaysay, the lowest income district in 1970 was the only one to substantially increase its planting of rice, accomplished by practically eliminating corn from its fields.

Number of Employed Persons per Household

It is characteristic of the peasant mode of production (Caldwell 1982) that, although all household members participate in farm work, only the head, who serves as owner–operator, has an "occupation." Others are classified, rather patronizingly, as "unpaid family workers." Confirming this observation, the 1970 survey disclosed that in Magsaysay there were only 1.43 employed persons per household; in Matanao, 1.34. Ten years later, these numbers had increased to 2.16 and 2.24 for the two sites, respectively.

The size of these gains is astonishing but they were accomplished by the same mechanism in both communities: the entry of women into paid (rather than unpaid) employment as a result of new opportunities. In 1970, only 16.6 women were employed per 100 households in Magsaysay and 21.6 in Matanao. By 1980, the values had risen to 92.8 and 94.6! The labour of adult males was also being used much more intensively. In 1970, men engaged in farm work were considered to be fully employed. A decade later, this assumption proved to be simplistic. By 1980, 24% of Magsaysay men who engaged in farming as their primary occupation, and 32% of those in Matanao, had secondary occupations as well. Almost all of the latter were in nonfarm sectors of the economy.

Growth of Nonfarm Small Business

The number and variety of business enterprises started between 1970 and 1980 have proven to be critical variables differentiating the growth patterns of the two communities. In Magsaysay, the total number of enterprises rose from 50 to 148. Major gains were in small convenience (*sari-sari*) stores (from 30 to 67), general merchandise stores (from 4 to 23), and farm-equipment rental firms (0 to 22). In Matanao, only a moderate expansion occurred (from 72 to 87 enterprises); there were slight gains in *sari-sari* stores (from 40 to 49) and equipment rentals (0 to 5), but the number of general merchandise stores was halved (19 to 10). The increasing importance of the rice trade can be gleaned from the addition of four new mills in each community, raising the total processing facilities from 5 to 13. These, like equipment services, were found in rural districts.

REVISION OF THE OCCUPATIONAL STRUCTURE

Occupational distributions from both communities were compiled in each survey. Over the decade, working men retained their commitment to on-farm agriculture — 70–80% of them in both municipalities without significant change. Blue-collar employment (artisans and craftworkers) held a distant second place in Matanao in 1970 (16%), whereas white-collar jobs (sales, clerical, and professional) were third with 11%. In Magsaysay, both blue- and white-collar males numbered only 8% of those at work when baseline data were collected.

By 1980 in Matanao, blue-collar workers made up only 8% of the total males and white-collar jobs were held by only 7%. Greater advancement in Magsaysay was indicated by the rise of white-collar workers to 9% whereas blue-collar jobs had fallen to 5% of the total. The changing work habits of women, however, explained the change in participation of household labour and in growth of enterprises noted previously.

In 1970, women formed a small part of the labour force (12–16%) in both municipalities and were concentrated in traditional jobs — sales, clerical, and teaching. By 1980, they had become 43% of all employed persons in both municipalities. A substantial proportion (21% in Magsaysay and 28% in Matanao) had been added to the ranks of farm labour, which now performed lighter physical work such as chemical spraying and machine tending.

The largest single addition of female labour (41% in Magsaysay and 37% in Matanao), however, took place in farm businesses other than raising crops, primarily raising livestock and poultry for market. The third category where women's employment increased over the decade was "sales" (20% in Magsaysay and 15% in Matanao). This category includes *sari-sari* storekeeping and other vending and peddling activities. During the decade, the commerce in both *poblaciones* expanded from weekly to daily market activities. With minor (white-collar) exceptions, all new employment for women was in informal sector commerce. In part, the amazing gains in women's employment may be explained by average improvements of 3–4 years of education.

The impact of population growth on the employment of children has been the source of much speculation. Where wages for farm labour decline, it has been assumed that households will add children to the work force to boost family earnings. In 1980, in Davao del Sur, however, the proportion of children aged 10–14 years who were employed was only 4% in Magsaysay and 7% in Matanao. That they were remaining in school is confirmed by the rising level of grade completion in both communities.

Change in Total Household Income

Annual cash income from all sources was recorded for each household in both survey years. When 1980 values are corrected for inflation, we find that the mean household income in Magsaysay increased from PHP 1711 to PHP 4860.[1] In Matanao, the comparable figures are PHP 1506 and PHP 3561. The adjusted annual municipal averages support the conclusion that purchasing power has improved by 2.8 times in Magsaysay and 2.4 times in Matanao since 1970.

Household income data also indicate that real earnings are being

---

[1]*In 1978, 7.41 Philippine pesos (PHP) = 1 U.S. dollar (USD).*

distributed with greater equity than in 1970. First, the divergent pattern of earnings separating *población* and rural locations has diminished sharply in both municipalities. When a measure of skewness (median/mean) is applied to the 10-year trend in each community, both sets of index values increase by an identical 10 points (0.55 to 0.65 in Magsaysay and 0.47 to 0.57 in Matanao).

Because the municipalities of Davao del Sur depend on crop production, the income gains described are based upon improved farming methods. Most of the advances are due to increased yield with high-yield rice varieties. The average harvest in 1970 was between 2 and 3 t/ha. In 1980, this value had risen to 4–5 t/ha. In addition, double-cropping during a single season had become the norm. Furthermore, the price of rice appears to have kept pace with inflation throughout the decade (IBRD 1980:198–199).

Diversification Hypothesis

The major finding of this longitudinal study from the point of view of development is that, in 1980, the residents of the two municipalities were supporting themselves twice as well as they had been 10 years earlier, in spite of the fact that, as a result of land reform, they cultivated only 60% of the land they had cultivated previously. The immediate explanation is to be found in the doubling of rice yields, the level of diversification present in both municipalities, and the fact that each municipality showed a distinct pattern of adaptive change in intensified participation in the labour force by household members.

Magsaysay pursued intensive rice cultivation with diversified small business activities related, in the main, to smallholder agriculture. An important role was assigned to women, who served both as farm labourers and informal sector entrepreneurs. Diversification in Matanao consisted of combining much-reduced subsistence cultivation of corn with expanded cash-cropping of sugar and coconut, together with plantation labour. Women worked in the fields in greater numbers than in Magsaysay, but were equally engaged in livestock and poultry raising and were only somewhat less active in informal sector trade.

Because household income distribution in Matanao is both more equal and more substantial than in 1970, no support can be found for the polarization hypothesis. However, the level of prosperity attained here, as reflected in mean household income, is only 75% of that in Magsaysay. Heavier dependence upon export commodities (cacao, coconut, coffee, and sugar) also builds instability into the Matanao economy.

DEMOGRAPHIC CHARACTERISTICS

Loss in Population and Gain in Median Age

Between 1970 and 1980, the average annual rate of population decline was 1.75%. The net loss was greater in Matanao (5610 to 4471, or 20%) than it was in Magsaysay (6529 to 5549, or 15%). At the time of the baseline study, the median age of both municipalities was only 14.7 years. By

1980, the Magsaysay median had risen to 17.5 years, whereas Matanao's had reached 18.6. An absolute decline in the 0–9 year age group was responsible for this, but there were also sharp declines in the survival ratios of the population aged 10–39 years in 1970. These data indicate the combination of outmigration and declining fertility. Whichever forces were at work, they were equally effective in the two communities.

Population Turnover

The 1980 households residing in the two municipalities are equal to the 1970 population minus departing households plus arriving households. Over the decade, 33.2% of Magsaysay and 27.6% of Matanao households left these municipalities. In-migrants replaced 51.6% of the net loss from Magsaysay and 49.6% from Matanao explaining the source of the absolute population decline noted in the preceding paragraph. The loss in both municipalities was highest (40% of 1970 households) from high-income farming areas suggesting displacement of former tenants. Conversely, the replacement rate was highest in the Magsaysay *población*, which became a concentration point for contract farm labour. The low-income farming districts in both towns retained the highest proportion (80%) of their 1970 households.

Fertility Declines

The crude birth rates (CBR expressed per 1000 population) measured in the Digos-Padada Valley in 1970 (45.8 in Magsaysay and 44.5 in Matanao) were equal to, but no greater than, those established for the rural Philippines by the National Demographic Survey. By 1978, however, family planning services had helped to reduce the national rural CBR to 34.2 (Hackenberg and Magalit 1985:xxvi) and, in 1980, the two towns of the Digos-Padada Valley had CBRs of 20.5 (Magsaysay) and 25.9 (Matanao). These local declines were twice the national average. The age-specific fertility rates among Magsaysay's married women in the 20–34 year age group were lower than those of Matanao. Consequently, the total fertility rate (TFR) of the former community (3.3) was significantly below that of the latter (4.1) in 1980; in the baseline study, both had TFRs of 7.5!

Acceptance of Family Planning

In 1970, national family planning was in a formative stage and contraceptive use was minimal. In 1973, for example, only 12% of rural married women were using any method (Concepción and Smith 1977:35). In 1978, rates of contraceptive use for four mostly rural regions outside Manila ranged from 30 (Southern Luzon) to 47% (Southern Mindanao) for all methods (Hackenberg and Magalit 1985:114). By 1980, however, the acceptance rate in the Digos-Padada Valley had risen to 56% for married women aged 15–44 years in both municipalities; 32% of whom were using effective methods (pills, intrauterine devices [IUDs], and tubal ligation). The greatest proportion of effective contraceptors (46%) appeared in the area of Magsaysay with high farm income.

Fertility Reduction

The proportion of younger women who chose early marriage shifted downward dramatically in the years after 1970. Sharpest declines, of 50% or more, appeared in the 15–24 year age groups. They were of greater magnitude in Magsaysay, where rates for ages 15–19 years fell from 23.8 to 6.0%, and for ages 20–24 years, from 69.5 to 34.2%; comparable declines for Matanao were from 11.2 to 6.1% and 55.7 to 33.6%.

Diversification in Development

Diversification implies income growth with increasing equity, based on substantial gains in agricultural productivity. The process has entailed changes in residence, education, employment, and household earning capacity, all of which have also provided a favourable environment for reduction in both early marriage and fertility. The Green Revolution in the Digos-Padada Valley has brought both of the major blessings of rural modernization: income gains and fertility losses. Regional trends have upended the Malthusian forecast of reinforcing relationships between poverty and population growth, terminating in "positive checks."

The Green Revolution has not always been so beneficial. In Southern Luzon, the same independent variables have generated two possible outcomes: stratification and polarization (Roumasset and Smith 1981; Kikuchi and Hayami 1983). In the former case, complex division of farm income among lessors and tenured labourers seems to produce the involutionary pattern of shared poverty described by Geertz (1963). In the latter case, a simplified division of farm income among a landowning elite and contract labourers produces the polarities of wealth for a few and misery for the rest.

How does Southern Mindanao differ from Southern Luzon? There are two basic determinants in the Digos-Padada Valley that may be absent elsewhere. First, a multicrop farm economy, mixing tenure types (plantation and homestead) and levels of investment (corporate agribusiness and owner-operated small holdings), has multiplied the cash flow through the area with consequent expansion and enrichment of the occupational structure and opportunities for rural small-business activities. Children of farm households have employment sources available other than a share of the family farming enterprise. Second, as mentioned earlier, family planning has been less effective in Southern Luzon, thus increasing pressure against income gains.

MECHANISMS OF CHANGE: FROM SELF-DIRECTION TO OTHER DIRECTION

The metamorphosis of peasant farmers into farm systems managers originates in the production prerequisites of high-yield variety cereals. There are essential complementarities between hybrid seeds, irrigation fertilizer, and increased labour (Barker and Cordova 1978; Wickham et al.

18

1978). If any essential factor is lacking, it becomes a constraint, increasing the gap between potential and actual yields (Herdt and Wickham 1978). To use the combined inputs on schedule, the farm operator becomes a credit consumer.

In the peasant society of the recent past, the landlord was the source of all inputs, including credit. But the patron–client bonds linking landlord and tenant have been broken by land reform (J.C. Scott 1976:209–210). To retain a place for the smallholder in the new land-tenure system, government agencies have entered the scene to provide the essentials formerly supplied by the landlord: irrigation, fertilizer, technical advice, and working capital. The landlord was the decision-maker in the old system. Today, he or she has been replaced by a phalanx of bureaucratic structures that, together, provide "other-direction" to the formerly self-directed producer–landowner.

The government has taken charge of private farming through agencies responsible for each of these essentials. Land is managed by the Ministry of Agrarian Reform (MAR). Water is controlled and allocated by the National Irrigation Administration (NIA). Subsidized credit throughout the 1970s was provided by Masagana 99, a crash program administered by technicians of the Bureau of Agricultural Extension (BAEX) through 240 rural branches of the Philippine National Bank. There were 636 000 borrowers during the 1st year of the program. By accepting Masagana credit, the farmer puts the land under the effective management of a BAEX farm technician, of whom there were 4000 in 1976 (IBRD 1976:176–180; Castillo 1983:183–257).

To participate in either land reform or Masagana credit allocation, a farm operator must join the government cooperative program, Samahang Nayon, which offers instruction in production technology and financial management. By 1979, there were over 933 500 members in 18 180 cooperatives (Castillo 1983:75–77). Applicants for credit must be certified by their MAR officer. A requirement for MAR certification is Samahang Nayon membership thus closing the bureaucratic ring.

The establishment and maintenance of this Orwellian quagmire of technocratic control requires financing. The cost of rice self-sufficiency, achieved in 1976, was met through astronomical foreign borrowings, which rose from slightly more than USD 0.2 billion/year at the beginning of the 1970s to more than USD 1.0 billion in 1978 and subsequent years (USAID 1980:37). This vicious cycle came to an end in 1983 when the Philippine government was no longer able to service its foreign debt of nearly USD 30 billion.

Precipitous fertility declines, like massive gains in rice productivity, were accomplished by a hierarchical structure of government agencies, an extension program staffed by field technicians reaching every *barrio*, and substantial foreign financing through development loans. The impact recorded in the preceding section was the achievement of the National Population and Family Planning Outreach Program (NPFPOP), begun in 1976. The key element was the establishment of direct contact with every married couple of reproductive age through a network of 2700 Full-time Outreach Workers (FTOWs) who acted as motivators, educators, and contraceptive suppliers. Contraceptives for NPFPOP were maintained at

45 332 *Barrio* Supply Points (BSPs) by mid-1980. The entire effort was coordinated by a lead agency, the Philippine Population Commission (POPCOM). In Davao del Sur in 1980, 47 FTOWs were at work and 726 BSPs were in operation.

Over the decade, the direct costs of this program reported by POPCOM (1978:78–79) were PHP 1.43 billion, or roughly USD 193 million, of which 60% was provided by the United States Agency for International Development (USAID). Beginning in 1980, a USD 50 million loan was provided by the World Bank and an additional USD 20 million came from the United Nations Fund for Population Activities to continue the POPCOM program. Under the crisis conditions prevailing in Philippine government finances since 1983, however, the level of support for program continuation remains uncertain.

In a recent review of Philippine government accomplishments during the 1970s (USAID 1980), three dangerous tendencies were noted: proliferation of government agencies, their uneven administrative capacity, and overly centralized decision-making and administrative control. However, as Gable and Springer (1979) observed, any development strategy such as rice self-sufficiency or population control that relies on science and technology in a developing country can be implemented only by a massive, centralized administrative effort.

Clearly, the first-stage development of these programs that showed miraculous successes is at an end. The second stage, if there is to be one, will require administrative units to achieve greater efficiency by adapting to local conditions rather than to national directives. For this purpose, most of the existing bureaucracy will become redundant. In their place, local research programs capable of solving environment-specific problems, as foreseen by Binswanger and Ruttan (1977), will be needed.

The effectiveness of any attempt at local program design will depend on local sources of funding and local capacity for decision-making through the process elsewhere described as microurbanization (Hackenberg 1984b). Should this become possible, each region's machinery for farm production and population control will begin to diverge from the others. Perhaps farmers and community groups can become partners in research, development, and decision-making. If so, diversification may prove to be the solution for both the government and the farm village under Green Revolution conditions — and the Malthusian forecast may remain upended.

20

Industrial Development and Rural Malay Households: Changing Strategies of Reproduction

Aihwa Ong

Agrarian Transition and Demographic Processes: Conceptual Framework

Among peasants of Sungai Jawa, a densely populated village in Peninsular Malaysia, a new strategy of subsistence has emerged, which represents a local shift in Malay population dynamics. This paper describes the postwar changes in rural economy and state policies that generated conditions under which Malay families developed new goals and alternative mechanisms to maximize opportunities for accumulating material and symbolic wealth. In particular, it examines how industrial development has intensified a break in rural subsistence patterns and the subsequent effects of new roles of rural men and women on their marriage aspirations and family formation.

Several studies of household demographic behaviour in contemporary agrarian societies have maintained that large rural families are the rational and intended outcomes of labour demands in technologically underdeveloped countries. In the 1970s, scholars using the "human capital" approach focused on the microprocesses of individual and family developmental cycles to argue that increasing rates of household demands for labour result in many children in Indian and Javanese peasant families (Mamdani 1973; White 1976).

Recently, this "value of children" model has been refashioned to account for demographic processes in situations of agrarian transition. Some scholars have noted that increasing capitalist demands for cheap and plentiful rural labour have helped sustain, not diminish, population growth in Third World countries. Thus, Meillassoux (1984) maintains that labour-exporting "domestic societies" in Africa experience profound insecurity because of the uncertainty of migrant remittances to rural families. In his view, "breaks" in the circulation of "family income" and market supplies bring about "a burst of natality as a means of social security" that ensures "the survival of the younger generations for longer periods."

Similarly, de Janvry (1981) argues that the survival strategies of "semiproletarianized peasants" in Latin American countries continue to favour large families. Land scarcity requires the dual household strategies of access to additional resources (in the cash economy) and "the overexploitation of family labour," which "inexorably" implies more children. Thus, even when poverty results in an increase of young out-migrants, their remittances enable rural families to be maintained at "optimum size."

Few of these generalizations are underpinned by microanalyses of actual communities that indicate how rural families deploy labour, share income, and control fertility in conditions of rapid social change. Both Meillassoux and de Janvry assume a universal agrarian response to capitalist requirements for labour whereby both capitalist enterprises and rural households are said to benefit, in different ways, from the production of a large number of children. This capital-deterministic model does not encompass the internal dynamics of rural society wherein different peasant strata may operate differently in conditions of capitalist development. Furthermore, such an approach excludes the possibility that different agrarian regions, subjected to different state policies, may experience alternative transformations, resulting in a diversity of demographic responses within the same country.

The present study of changing demographic behaviour in the peasant-to-worker transition assumes that there is no universal demographic outcome resulting from the encounter between capitalist development and agrarian societies. Taking domestic groups and communities as culturally constituted (rather than statistically conceived) entities in specific historical contexts, it is argued that quantitative measures of human behaviour must be subjected to qualitative analysis, focusing on relations within domestic groups, the society, the economy, and the state. Furthermore, because agrarian transition is often attended by increasing social differentiation within rural society, a class-specific analysis of strategies of reproduction will help identify alternative patterns of family formation. It is insufficient to discuss the *biological* reproduction of individuals as microprocesses separate from the *social* reproduction of their relations of consumption and production. The particular mode of integrating Malay peasants into the labour market under monopoly capitalism places limits on the "human capital" model of household strategies. Divergent cultural norms and the varied forms of political–economic integration of different groups into the wider society mean that the demographic picture derived from single-village studies cannot be automatically assumed to reflect national population trends.

STATE AND SOCIAL ENGINEERING OF THE MALAY COMMUNITY

Malaysia is perhaps not unique among Third World countries in the degree to which state agencies influence the social and demographic behaviour of an ethnic group. Since the end of colonial rule, Peninsular (or West) Malaysia has continued to supply the world markets with tin as well as rubber and palm oil produced in plantations and peasant smallholdings.

In 1970, Malays who, together with aboriginal groups, claim native status in the country as "sons-of-the-soil" (*bumiputra*) constituted 53% of the total Peninsular population of over 9 million. About 36% of the population was made up of ethnic Chinese, and the rest of Indians, who were employed mainly in the urban and plantation sectors. As rice peasants, smallholding farmers, and fishers, about 85% of Malays lived in the countryside where half of the population subsisted below the poverty level (Malaysia 1976a:72).

In 1969, an explosion of communal rioting focused national attention on the plight of rural Malays, causing the state to intervene in capitalist development and social engineering. A New Economic Policy (NEP) was formulated in 1971 to "restructure society" and "eradicate poverty" by changing the demographic distribution so that the multiethnic composition of Malaysian society became "visibly reflected in its countryside and towns, farms and factories, shops and offices" (Malaysia 1976a:9).

Indeed, by the late 1960s, conditions in the countryside were already generating an expanding population of young Malay men and women increasingly unable, or disinclined, to make a living from agricultural production. Annual population growth among Malays was 2.8%, and cultural preference for nuclear family organization kept the average household size at five persons (Malaysia 1981:72–74). Population pressure on parental property and land accumulation by the new rural elite increased land hunger in rural society. Meanwhile, the postwar introduction of free, compulsory primary education, complemented by automatic promotion to secondary education in 1964, increased the number of peasant young people who were being channeled into occupations outside the *kampung* (village) society. In the following decades, outmigration from the village by male and, increasingly, female secondary school leavers grew, adding to the pool of urban unemployed. In 1970, Malays constituted only 15% of the urban population; however, 10 years later, they formed over 20% (Malaysia 1981:229).

This sustained urban migration coincided with the state-sponsored export-industrialization program that, within a single decade, established 59 industrial estates for manufacturing plants set up by multinational subsidiaries and local companies. In 1979, the Home Affairs Minister confirmed that the "urban drift" of rural Malays was "a deliberate . . . societal engineering strategy" within the framework of the NEP. The "rural–agricultural sector," he pointed out, was "the major reservoir [of labour power] . . . for economic development" (Anonymous 1979).

This large-scale shift of Malays from the primary to the secondary sector is reflected in labour-force statistics. Between 1970 and 1980, the labour force in agriculture declined from more than 53% of the total working population to 41%. During the same period, the percentage of workers in manufacturing rose from 8 to 16 (Malaysia 1981:229). In 1976, the state required hundreds of multinational companies in Malaysia to have a 33%

bumiputra representation in their labour force. About 60 000 of these new industrial workers were Malay women from rural villages (Ariffin 1980). The government expected that, by 1985, the number of production workers would exceed that of agricultural workers by 35 to 31% in the industrializing Malaysian economy (Malaysia 1981:229).

This occupational shift of rural Malays, in conjunction with the state-administered transfer of the nation's wealth, in the form of trust agencies, to the *bumiputra* population to "create a commercial and industrial community among the *bumiputra* is the core of the NEP program" (Malaysia 1981:63). Such direct state intervention into the process of class formation unquestionably shapes and conditions shifts in Malay household dynamics and population trends at the local level. We have used Kuala Langat, a rural district south of the Klang industrial belt, to investigate the demographic consequences of proletarianization in a Malay cash-cropping village.

MALAY SOCIETY IN KUALA LANGAT: RURAL DIFFERENTIATION

Kuala Langat is a coastal district of 83 300 ha lying south of Port Klang, the major port in Peninsular Malaysia. During the colonial period (1876–1957), the heavily forested coastal strip was opened by immigrant Malays who established *kampung* settlements in the interstices of tin-mining camps, new marketing towns, and the nascent plantation economy. By World War II, Malay *kampung* society was composed of a solid core of independent peasant producers, their farm size varying within the small range of 1.5–4.0 ha. Already, on the fringe of village society were groups of landless peasants, many of whom engaged in clandestine cutting of forest reserves, although their subsistence was primarily dependent upon casual day labour in the wider economy.

In the 15 years after independence in 1957, Malay population growth, changing land use, and the greater integration of the district within the national system, accelerated rural differentiation. In 1970, there were 107 170 persons in the district, over 50% of them Malays (Malaysia 1972:81). Throughout the decade, smallholders had to compete with plantation and urban development for land, while experiencing a decline in farm productivity because of aging tree crops. Thus, smallholding area declined from 22 600 to 18 500 ha between 1966 and 1978. As rubber prices plummeted in the late 1960s and early 1970s, more rubber holdings were converted to coconut and interplanted with coffee, cocoa, and oil palms.

Meanwhile, as part of the state development effort, the penetration of government agencies, projects, and educational institutions into village society promoted the rise of a white-collar rural elite. With an external (and relatively substantial) source of income, teachers and civil servants ensconced in rural townships could compete with peasants for land in the Malay Reservations. (These areas were designated during the colonial period as land set aside for Malay ownership; non-Malays could not

24

purchase such lands. In independent Malaysia, many rural Malays have been able to hold onto their holdings only because of this legal protection from non-Malay capital.) Direct state intervention has also helped forge a "free" Malay rural proletariat out of the landless, underemployed population accumulating in *kampung* society.

In the mid-1970s, the green, plantation *kampung* character of the district was broken by the insertion of a small Free Trade Zone (FTZ), a "rural industrialization project" that was expected to "put the vast pool of rural manpower to good use" (Malaysia 1976b:19). The subsidiaries of three Japanese electronics and small-machine companies set up plants in labour-intensive production activities for which few skills were required. Young village women, hitherto reluctant to leave *kampung* environs, could now commute daily on bicycles or in buses to the FTZ, while continuing to live with their *kampung* families. By 1975, the FTZ had a total labour force of 2000 of whom 90% were female production workers and clerks. A few village men were employed as manual labourers, packers, and security guards. More senior staff members were recruited from outside the district and country.

Throughout the late 1970s, as more rural Malays participated in wage relations in the Klang industrial belt and in the local FTZ, *kampung* households exhibited significant differentials in landholdings, access to wage earnings, and general material wealth. In contrast to other regions in Malaysia, where "Green Revolution" programs have had the effect of "repeasantizing" dislocated or impoverished Malays, state intervention into Kuala Langat accentuated uneven proletarianization whereby a reduced core of self-employed peasants struggled to exist alongside an incipient landlord-cum-bureaucratic class. This process of differentiation among village households is not merely the cyclical effect of the family developmental cycle but rather the consequence of alternative reproductive strategies through which households attempt to secure their social position through reordering family processes.

A different picture of the local effects of "Green Revolution" is presented by Kahn (1983). In Negri Sembilan, Kahn observes that technological inputs have enabled poor farmers to consolidate their household position as viable peasant enterprises, thus preserving or even recreating a class of peasants rather than inducing proletarianization.

Changing Peasant Household Strategies in the Study Village

The field work for this study was conducted in 1979–1980 in a large Malay Reservation of over 800 ha, *kampung* Sungai Jawa (a pseudonym) in Kuala Langat. The village is situated in the northern half of the district, about 10 km from the FTZ and the nearest rural township; it is also linked by trunk road to Port Klang 24 km to the north, and to Kuala Lumpur about 65 km away. A random household sample of 242 domestic groups (out of a total of 750 households) revealed wide differentials in land ownership and an occupational shift, by household head and by generation, from self-employment in peasant activities to wage employment outside the *kampung* economy. Such quantitative indicators, it is argued,

25

reveal a change in village household function vis-à-vis the wider society and reflect alternative strategies of subsistence.

Rural differentiation in Sungai Jawa involves simultaneous processes of proletarianization and peasantization. The household sample (Table 1) indicates that over 60% of *kampung* households have been, or are being, separated from their means of production. Landless peasants, sometimes having only a house lot, sell their labour for a living, but seldom enjoy the security of permanent employment. Land-poor households constitute the largest peasant fraction (38%). Their smallholdings do not yield sufficient income for family subsistence and members have to pick up supplementary wages for consumption, with little left over for savings. Small peasants (25% of the total population) operate viable farms of 0.8–2.0 ha that provide them with relative independence from the wage market. The middle and rich households, including farmers and salaried workers (who own holdings of 4–30 ha) enjoy sufficient farm income, occasionally hire day labourers, accumulate land, and are well placed to dominate the local land market.

This process of "uneven proletarianization" is further illuminated if we look at the distribution of principal occupations of household heads (Table 2). Although 19% of household heads have remained self-employed peasant producers, 35% seek temporary wage employment as their major economic activity. The percentage of household heads who are members of the incipient rural bourgeoisie is small: a handful of landlords, traders, and salaried workers who have access to secure salaries, government subsidies, and contacts by which to accumulate wealth and prestige.

To what extent are differentials in land ownership and occupations merely an effect of individual and family cycles, and not a consequence of class determinations? If land access and work status are effects of hard work and advancement throughout a peasant's life, then one would expect that a villager embarking on householding would pass through the successive statuses of (landless) farm labourer, peasant producer, and, in rare cases, landlord. However, in Sungai Jawa, household heads in landless and land-poor categories are mainly in their mid- to late-40s and wage labour is not just a stage in their life-cycle but a life-long activity.

More definitive evidence of class determination of household differentiation is the inability of most peasants in these strata to gain access to land and thus to enhance the prospects for their offspring. Islamic inheritance rules fragment already small holdings into what are, at most, house lots and kitchen gardens, providing children with a residual

Table 1. Distribution of households by amount of land owned.

Stratum	Farm size (ha)	Households		Total area	
		Number	%	Hectares	%
Landless	0.0–0.2	57	23.5	4.1	1.3
Land-poor	0.2–0.8	91	37.6	53.4	16.4
Small	0.8–2.0	65	26.9	91.5	28.2
Middle	2.0–4.0	13	5.4	37.2	11.4
Rich	4.0–30.0	16	6.6	138.8	42.7
Total		242	100.0	325.0	100.0

Table 2. *Primary occupations of household heads.*

	Number	%
Self-employed peasants		
Peasant producers	47	19.4
Village professionals (native midwives and spirit healers)	5	2.1
Market agents	12	5.0
Total	64	26.5
Temporary workers		
Day labourers and sharecroppers	68	28.1
Contract workers	17	7.0
Total	85	35.1
Permanent workers		
Government labourers	44	18.1
Industrial labourers	13	5.4
Total	57	23.5
Landlords and entrepreneurs		
Entrepreneurs	9	3.7
Landlords	5	2.1
Total	14	5.8
Government white-collar employees		
Teachers and clerks	8	3.3
Police and soldiers	5	2.1
Total	13	5.4
Unemployed and retired	9	3.7
Total	242	100.0

anchorage in *kampung* society. Family wage workers make about MYR 100–400/month,[1] earnings that are directly consumed by the family. Even with careful budgeting, few can aspire to buy land, particularly in conditions of rising real-estate prices. In the late 1970s, an undeveloped 1.2-ha (3-acre) holding cost MYR 8000. In less attractive locales, a similar holding planted with oil palm seedlings commanded MYR 17 000; in Sungai Jawa, it cost about MYR 24 000. Over the decades, landless villagers have tended to migrate to the cities or have been resettled on government land schemes elsewhere in the country.

In Sungai Jawa, however, this process has not been unilaterally fragmenting; individual cases have shown upward mobility. A few young men from poor families, having benefited from some years of education, have been able to obtain permanent wage employment, working, for example, as stevedores, and have been able to purchase small farms and return to peasant production. Others who have become teachers and bureaucrats may start out with no land but over the years accumulate village holdings, allowing them to enter the ranks of the middle to rich farmers.

Such individual career paths are indicative of a major shift in the relationship between *kampung* society and the wider economy. Thus, although small, middle, and rich peasants, unlike the village poor, have the material bases to remain in the peasant strata, they aspire to other levels. Different peasant groups are raising their children to become semiskilled and white-collar workers bound for the capitalist labour market. Significant numbers of the younger generation are, therefore, coming of age as wage workers who do not engage in any kind of agricultural activities.

[1] *All cash amounts are in 1979 prices; 2 Malaysian ringgits (MYR) = 1 U.S. dollar (USD).*

Malays are fond of saying "Each child has his [her] own fortune" (*tiap tiap anak ada rezekinya*). In Sungai Jawa, at least, this "fortune" has important implications for family planning and social change. The future roles of children are no longer the outcome of habitual instruction and practices, but rather the product of new family aspirations, individual effort, and state agencies in the socialization and deployment of rural labour. *Kampung* households, depending on their social position, are differently facilitated and limited by their abilities to place sons and daughters on alternative career paths rarely traveled by their parents. For the rural poor, new occupations in the wage labour market arise out of the exigencies of survival in a situation of land scarcity. For the well-off families, on the other hand, alternative career paths are more clearly charted out by the school system and state bureaucratic structures that provide the most assured channels of upward mobility for *kampung* people.

A closer look at the shifts in occupation between generations in different peasant categories reveals that, in following educational opportunities and strategic contacts, poorer peasant households begin with a handicap of competing uses for limited resources (Table 3). Thus, although there is a high rate of retention of grown children (over 18 years old) in almost all peasant groups, the poorer peasants keep grown children at home more as wage earners than as dependants being groomed for careers outside the peasant sector. Among the landless and land-poor families, 60% of children over 18 years old have dispersed, all of them living outside the subdistrict. Among those who have remained in their parents' households, 7 of 24 grown children work as rural labourers. The rest, especially daughters, are employed as wage workers in the new industries. Two children are government servants. The landless families seldom tolerate "idle" grown children who are still in school or looking for work. Such dependants are not encouraged to remain at home.

Among the land-poor peasants who still operate farms, 60% of the children, most of them daughters, are in industrial and service employment. A few have found government employment. As the largest peasant fraction in Sungai Jawa, the land-poor households, by supporting more of their children through high school, hope to avoid descending into the ranks of rural paupers.

The "small peasantry" with 0.8–2.0 ha of land is also tending to disperse. Although it has sufficient resources to support dependent children, the small peasantry attempts to keep its children out of peasant

Table 3. Retention and dispersal of children 18 years and over, by peasant stratum.

Stratum	Households with children	Children				
		At home		Left home		
		Number	%	Number	%	Total
Landless	15	24	40	36	60	60
Land-poor	60	108	40	161	60	269
Small	49	91	42	126	58	217
Middle	10	25	78	7	22	32
Rich	14	26	37	44	63	70
Total	148	274	42	374	58	648

production and instead to promote their entry into the new professions, especially district-level administration. In small peasant households, only 11 out of 91 grown children engage in any kind of agricultural work; 30% are still in school or unemployed and 40% are industrial and service workers. Significantly, a small proportion (7%) of the children hold white-collar jobs. A few unemployed, unmarried daughters are living at home.

Finally, among the better-off strata, the children have generally avoided agricultural work and have been more successful in gaining footholds in the state bureaucratic system: 15% of children from the middle peasantry and 13% from the rich are in government employment. Compared to the children of poorer households, only about 30% of such offspring engage in wage work. Besides those supported by parents at home, significant proportions of the children of the rural elite have received government scholarships, left the village, and live in vocational boarding schools and colleges.

DAUGHTERS AND SONS: WAGE EMPLOYMENT AND HOUSEHOLD REPRODUCTION

In the generalized "commoditization" of *kampung* society, the "fortune" of children is not only redefined, but also differentiated from that of the parents. The subsistence base of most rural households no longer depends upon unpaid family labour controlled by the household head, but rather upon the sale of labour by household members. Mass education has also helped change the attitude of most peasant families toward wage employment outside *kampung* society. Most village young people dislike and often refuse to do farm work. In fact, the life cycle of rural boys now begins with schooling, followed by wage employment, much like that of urban youth. Those who revert to smallholding agriculture do so only as an activity supplementary to wage work. For village daughters, their life cycles are more varied; they pass from domestic chores to school, temporary wage employment, increased household responsibilities, and then marriage. Although most sons and daughters over 18 years old eventually leave their parents' households, they do so for different reasons. Among the poor, children leave to become wage earners or to establish their own households, whereas the offspring of the well-to-do leave to continue education in towns.

Thus, a major problem for household subsistence is parents' loss of control over children's labour, the fruits of that labour, and thus of parental authority. This loss of control over family labour is accentuated by increased family dependence on the cash incomes that children earn outside the village economy. Parental authority is weakened by the need to extract cash contributions from children whose labour and earnings are no longer at their disposal. Sons are especially resistant to sharing their earnings with family members. Children who work as migrant workers seldom remit regular amounts of money home, because the cost of urban living and transport often wipe out their meagre gains. Even those living at home frequently fail to share their earnings with the family. In Sungai Jawa, about 40% of grown sons and daughters live at home and commute to work in the Klang Valley or to the local FTZ. Nevertheless, working sons in particular resist regular pooling of their income in the household budget. They argue that private savings are necessary because they cannot expect to inherit enough property to start an independent household after marriage.

Unmarried daughters prove more amenable to parental pressures to share the results of their labour with family members. As the father's authority over sons weakens, the mother's influence over the disposition of daughters' earnings becomes critical for day-to-day household sustenance. As the father's role of instructing sons in the *kampung* livelihood declines, mothers continue to train daughters in housework and child care, and they instill in them a primary role and responsibility in providing for the daily consumption needs of the family. Young working women are easily prevailed upon to contribute regularly to kitchen expenses.

In Sungai Jawa, most daughters working in the local FTZ contribute 50–70% of their wages to household budgets. Besides, they often pay the school expenses of younger siblings. By contrast, the cash contributions of sons are usually more limited (about 25% or less of their earnings) and variable, contingent upon their various personal needs as opposed to family claims. Nevertheless, the ability of mothers to mobilize a portion of children's earnings enables landless and land-poor families to maintain apparently "traditional" forms of cooperation in a situation of increasing economic individualization. Daughters from well-to-do households, by contrast, spend their earnings on personal items and set up savings accounts for future needs.

Thus the rustic appearance of Sungai Jawa, like many rural communities in the Asian countryside, disguises extensive dependence of rural households upon wage earnings and capitalist relations of production for daily survival. Furthermore, mothers have emerged as key figures in the partial collectivization of earnings, while unmarried daughters have become important foci in the new domestic arrangements. Time allocation surveys by age–gender categories showed that young women aged 16–24 years, most of whom are single, spend longer working (an average 9.2 hours/day) than young men (7.0 hours). Of all family members, daughters spend the most time working, whereas sons spend the least. Furthermore, among women in all age groups, factory workers work longer than nonwage workers (Table 4). Both the unpaid domestic activities of women and the wage earnings of unmarried daughters underpin the physical and social subsistence of the rural system. These new

Table 4. Average labour time (hours) of female factory workers and other women.

	Women workers	
	Factory	Others
Household chores	2.28	5.73
Farm work	0.42	0.99
Wage work	7.54	0.00
Total	10.24	6.72

domestic strategies have altered not only traditional patterns of domestic consumption but also attitudes toward marriage and fertility among the younger generation.

WOMEN WORKERS, DELAYED MARRIAGES, AND FERTILITY DECLINE

An immediate and calculated result of industrial wage employment for men and women in Sungai Jawa is a rising trend in age at first marriage. In the early 1960s, village women were married in their late teens; however, after the introduction of the FTZ factories, age at first marriage began to rise appreciably for women. For example, in 1978 and 1979, among employed women, the average age at marriage at the national level was 23 years. In parts of Malaysia that are not so well integrated into the national economy, *kampung* girls are still married in their teens. Laderman (1983:13) reports that young women in Kampung Mechang, coastal Trengganu, marry in their mid to late teens and that the median age at first pregnancy is 16 years old.

It is equally important that the marriage age among young women not involved in wage work is also rising, but at a slightly lower rate than among factory women. Among men, only those who have employment, or property, can afford to marry, and thus there is a slight fluctuation in their ages at first marriage. The overall trend in delaying marriage is related to mass education as well as the generalization of wage employment as the basic source of livelihood.

In particular, the contributions of young women toward domestic sustenance result in the postponement of marriage. Decisions to marry are frequently made in consultation with mothers and are carefully adjusted to family contingencies such as the education of siblings, the possibility of replacement by a wage-earning sibling, and the need for sufficient savings for a wedding. Although young men tend to withhold earnings from the family, their accumulation of funds toward the future establishment of their own households also delays marriage. Children of well-off families often postpone marriage to complete training for bureaucratic jobs or await suitable marital matches with members of urban-professional families.

Thus, in Sungai Jawa, family claims on the earnings of children, as well as individual career and marriage plans, contribute to a trend in delayed marriages that is approaching the national pattern. Improved rural health facilities throughout the country have helped sustain a high overall growth rate of 2.7% for the Malay population. It is expected that future declines in the Malay fertility rate will result not from any further rise in the marriage age of women, but rather from a change in attitudes regarding desirable family size (Malaysia 1981:212–218).

In Sungai Jawa, the increasing participation of young women in factory employment before marriage is accompanied by changing attitudes toward childbearing and family formation. Older women who came of age before the advent of large-scale female participation in the industrial labour market have had, on average, 6.5 children (Table 5). Given the demand for farm work and the need to balance the producer–consumer ratio in the peasant economy, these older women had spaced their children, at roughly 3-year intervals, over the course of their full reproductive cycles.

In dramatic contrast, young *kampung* women who have had at least 6 years schooling and some factory experience marry later and choose their own spouses. They claim to want no more than four children; most desire just a boy–girl pair within the first 5 years of marriage. They expect to spend the rest of their fertile years raising these children, helping with their school work, and perhaps returning to wage employment themselves. Although not publicly admitted, modern family-planning methods are used ("the pill" and intrauterine device [IUD]). The younger generation, although raised in rural society, see little or no future in *kampung* occupations; many are marrying late and having fewer children. Among families still fortunate enough to have some land, parents have come to view village holdings as future house lots for their children who reside in the village but sell their labour elsewhere.

These economic and social changes within rural Malay society not only enforce new considerations in the reproductive behaviour of the labouring population, but they can also disrupt the stability of marriages. Thus, long-term migrant work, job uncertainty, and changing values often break marital relations and disrupt the reproductive cycles of women. In Kuala Langat, divorce has increased substantially among young men and women engaged in wage employment, but this is also partly attributable to the young age structure of the population in the area. The district *Kadi* (Islamic judge) reports that, over the past decade, most of the divorces have had their origin in conflicts over money, including the pooling of earnings for household maintenance, contributions to parents-in-law, and changing consumer habits, such as drug taking (Table 6). Migrant men are often remiss in sending remittances home. They may set up polygamous unions in different places, thus multiplying the claims on their meagre incomes.

In FTZs throughout the Peninsula, an increasing number of women workers are young Malay divorcees, some of whom have small children. Migrant women, experiencing constant moves, the cost of urban living,

Table 5. Mean number of children ever-born to ever-married women.

Age group (years)	Children ever-born (number)	Women (number)
15–19	1.50	2
20–24	2.25	8
25–29	3.14	26
30–34	4.85	38
35–39	6.50	28
40–44	6.20	55
45–49	6.55	24
50–54	6.90	20
55–59	6.45	17
60–64	6.60	10
over 64	5.90	10

Table 6. Distribution (%) of reasons for Malay divorces in Kuala Langat, 1969–1979.

Year	Nonsupport by husband	Incompatibility	Interference by family	Extramarital relations		Other reasons[a]	Number of divorces
				Husband	Wife		
1969	40	30	10	10	5	5	46
1970	35	35	15	7	5	3	51
1971	30	40	20	5	5	0	56
1972	45	35	5	10	5	0	53
1973	45	30	5	10	7	3	62
1974	25	30	15	10	5	10	51
1975	43	35	10	5	2	5	78
1976	44	30	6	10	5	5	72
1977	45	30	15	15	3	2	59
1978	40	25	30	3	2	0	91
1979	45	15	15	10	15	5	76

Source: Adapted from the records of Kadi Mohammad Shari b. Ismail, Pejabat Islam, Sungai Manggis.
[a] These cases include impotence, sterility, nonconsummation of marriage, desire to take another wife, and husband's drug addiction.

unstable unions with men, and new consumer needs, are more likely than village women to use contraceptives regularly and to have fewer children. A survey of ever-married migrant women in their 20s conducted between 1971 and 1974 showed that migrants had an average of 1.9 children/woman, as compared to nonmigrants who averaged 3.1 children/woman. Whereas migrants had a fertility of only 60% of nonmigrants in general, migrants' fertility was half that of nonmigrants for women 20–24 years old (de Vanzo 1981).

Single working women who postpone marriage may form a variety of unions with men, in preparation for marriage or for economic security. Although premarital sexual activity has increased among wage workers, occasionally resulting in pregnancies, extramarital births have not become a noticeable trend. For the thousands of Malay women working in cities, a combination of individual economic survival and materialistic values has kept their fertility low, especially in conditions of frequent separations and a high probability of divorce.

Finally, the state, religious groups, and factories have intervened directly to control the sexual behaviour of Malay working men and women. Members of the Islamic fundamentalist (*dakwah*: missionary) movement call for "spiritual struggle" against individualistic Western values and state religious officers are empowered to arrest and punish Malay couples, not married to each other, caught in sexually compromising situations. The threat of moralistic and legal sanctions, particularly directed at vulnerable young women, has curtailed their participation in the urban "youth culture" and sent many flocking to join the *dakwah* movement. Donning heavy Middle Eastern robes, young Malay women observe strict segregation of the sexes. Their "cult of purity" and stress on "honest work" is a defensive reaction against charges of un-Islamic behaviour and moral laxity. Some factories, in response to workers' demands, have instituted Islamic classes to discourage extramarital sexual activity. (For a more extensive treatment of this theme, see Ong [in press]). Eager to extend their influence to marital relations, a few factories have slipped in family-planning classes. Mobile family-planning vans tour FTZs and the cheap living quarters of factory women dispensing free contraceptives. In short, growing surveillance by dominant factions of society intensifies labour discipline and sexual repression, curtailing extramarital activity and fertility increase among the nascent Malay working class.

CONCLUSION

In conclusion, it cannot be assumed that the local and regional effects of economic development on Malay class formation, family reproductive strategies, and individual aspirations will automatically lead to a decline in national population growth. Recently, Malaysia adopted the view that sustained development is critically dependent upon population growth and announced its goal to dramatically increase the current national population of 14 million to 70 million by the end of the century.

As the influx of rural Malays into manufacturing and service industries continues unabated, the government is encouraging, with support from plantation and industrial interests, the "informal" immigration of Indonesians and Muslim Philippinos who can be easily assimilated into *bumiputra* status. In 1984, Indonesian and Philippino immigrants constituted 37% of workers in agriculture and 16% of the labour force in manufacturing. There are an estimated 430 000 Indonesian workers in the country and many are settling. Immigration by potential *bumiputra* populations is expected to promote sustained population growth, without upsetting the carefully orchestrated ethnic composition of the country. In effect, the state has channeled local Malays into the industrializing and urban sectors of the economy, while allowing immigrants to provide a continuing supply of labour for agriculture and other primary industries.

If we review the changing reproductive practices among a local variant of the expanding Malay proletariat, we can see how arguments about child labour and household survival strategies in other Third World countries are not applicable.

Rural conditions in Malaysia enable even the poorest families to survive without extreme self-exploitation and child labour is no longer critical to farm production. In parts of Malaysia, changing rural household strategies, oriented toward urban and industrial employment, is facilitated by state policies that favour such aspirations among Malays. As more households come to depend on wage earnings rather than peasant production for daily maintenance and generational reproduction, children are raised to be workers in various capitalist markets and in the state bureaucracy. The authority of *kampung* fathers is eroded as sons struggle to make their own living apart from family claims. Mothers emerge as important agents guiding daughters into wage employment, handling their earnings for household needs, delaying their marriage plans, and providing child-care services should married daughters return to work.

Thus, in regions undergoing rapid economic change, the large-scale industrial employment of young rural women has effectively broken familial (and male) control of women's sexuality and fertility, and foreign cultural influences and intensified state interventions foster new attitudes toward consumerism, sexual repression, and family formation. Meanwhile, despite declining fertility among the emergent Malay proletariat, alternative state policies to recruit immigrant labour will probably contribute to high overall population growth.

DEMOGRAPHIC IMPACT OF RURAL DEVELOPMENT IN BANGLADESH

Barkat-e-Khuda

During the past century, much of the world has experienced economic development accompanied by a dramatic decline of mortality and fertility — a process referred to as the demographic transition. Although fertility decline (and other demographic changes such as increased age at marriage and higher levels of contraceptive use) has long been recognized as one of the consequences of industrialization and urbanization, almost every country that has experienced substantial rural development has also experienced fertility decline in rural areas (Kocher 1973). This chapter examines the impact of rural development on demographic change in Bangladesh, based on evidence from a village in Comilla-Kotwali Thana where rural development programs were initiated in the early 1960s by the Bangladesh Academy for Rural Development.

STUDY AREA

At the beginning of the Academy's program, Comilla-Kotwali Thana had economic problems similar to those found in other parts of the country. In 1961, population density in Comilla-Kotwali Thana was 784 persons/km^2 compared with 356 for the country as a whole, and the average farm size was only 0.69 ha compared with 1.42 for Bangladesh.

Smith (1979:17) observed that economic conditions had grown so harsh in some of the most flood-prone villages near Comilla that farmers had to sell their bullocks and were attempting to heave wooden ploughs through the soil with the force of their emaciated limbs. Women had to sell their jewelry, one of the most important liquid assets for a peasant family.

Like the rest of the country, Comilla-Kotwali Thana had a poor education system. The curriculum and school structure were inadequate: only about 20% of the population aged 5 years and above was literate in 1959.

The Comilla Program

The Comilla program began in 1959 with the establishment of the Pakistan Academy for Rural Development, which later became the Bangladesh Academy for Rural Development (BARD). The Academy was established by the government as an experiment in which development programs were conducted on a pilot scale to assess the feasibility of eventual adoption at the national level. The main aim of the Academy's program was to devise ways of increasing the agricultural production of ordinary cultivators, both to improve their incomes and to enlarge the food supply of the nation (Schuman 1967:3).

The Academy involved local farmers in a broad-based integrated rural development program that included agricultural extension; credit cooperatives; introduction of improved varieties of paddy and supplementary inputs such as irrigation, fertilizers, and pesticides; development of rural physical infrastructure; rural education; involvement of women in productive activities; and family planning. The integrated program in Comilla-Kotwali included the Cooperative Project and Experiment in Agricultural Extension, the Rural Works Programme, the Thana Irrigation Programme, Pilot Experiment in Rural Education, the Women's Programme, and the Family Planning Pilot Project. Of these, only the family-planning project is described here as it relates most closely to the subject of this chapter.

The Family Planning Programme was designed to promote the non-clinical distribution of contraceptives. It was administered by Academy faculty staff and the Thana Family Planning Officer. Women organizers from each village attended training sessions at the Academy and then passed on their knowledge to other women. The women who were trained were generally the traditional village midwives, who were entrusted with the responsibility of promoting family planning, distributing supplies, and keeping records of purchases. In 1964, the program was expanded to allow for the commercial distribution of contraceptives by male shopkeepers and others. Various steps were taken to publicize and motivate people to practice contraception.

Perhaps the most important effect of the Academy's programs was the increase in agricultural production and income. All available evidence shows that production in Thana grew significantly faster than district or country production. In addition, the program in Comilla created favourable preconditions for the introduction of high-yielding varieties (HYV) of crops and improvements in yields. At the beginning of the program, yields in Comilla-Kotwali Thana were 20% higher than district and national values. By the late 1960s, Thana yields were up to twice district and national yields and, by the mid-1970s, they were more than twice as high (Mueller and Anderson 1982:15). Interestingly, knowledge of improvements in agricultural yields was not confined to cooperative members but spread quickly among nonmembers as well.

The program stressed the interdependence between social and economic development. The proportion of literates in Comilla-Kotwali Thana rose from about 20% in 1959 to 40% by mid-1966 (Raper 1970:188), a substantial gain in the literacy level. Similar improvements in communication resulted from the spread of roads. The number of vehicles increased, facilitating contact with the outside world. Rahim (1971:22) reported an increase in the ownership of radios, clocks, and other modern items by cooperative members. The Women's Programme facilitated communication between women and promoted modern values. Women began to leave their homes regularly to meet other women.

There is no evidence to suggest that female age at marriage was different in Comilla-Kotwali Thana from the rest of the country when the program began. Contraceptive use in the early 1960s was similar to the national level (practiced by about 4% of the couples). Further, it appears that fertility levels in Comilla-Kotwali Thana were higher than the national averages in the late 1950s and early 1960s. In 1958–1959, total fertility rate (TFR) in Comilla-Kotwali Thana was 8.53; it began to decline in the 1960s and, by 1966–1967, it had dropped to 6.21, a decline of 27% (Stoeckel and Chowdhury 1973).

Comilla-Kotwali Thana, being exposed to rural development programs undertaken on a reasonable scale over a relatively long period, thus provided a particularly suitable area for this study.

METHODOLOGY

The nature of demographic change and of the conditions that bring about such change in rural agrarian societies cannot be adequately understood by relying exclusively upon large-scale cross-sectional surveys. It can be better understood by undertaking an in-depth microlevel study. The methodology employed here combined participant observation and collection of quantitative data through questionnaires. A detailed discussion on the methodology of data collection is given by Khuda (forthcoming).

The fieldwork was spread over 19 months from October 1979 to April 1981 and involved several phases. Two types of surveys were undertaken: a census enumeration of households and highly focused smaller surveys. The census survey included a household census, and surveys on landholdings, *aman* (rice crop) production, and labour force. The smaller surveys focused on nuptiality, family planning, the "value" of children, breastfeeding, household structure, time use, income and expenditure, and the nature of rural institutions. The census surveys were based on 100% enumeration, but the focused smaller surveys covered between 50 and 75% of all households, stratified according to cultivable area of landholding and other sampling criteria appropriate to the particular topic. In addition, vital events were continuously recorded during the entire period of fieldwork.

FINDINGS IN THE STUDY VILLAGE

Keeping in mind the objectives of the study, a village where rural-development programs had been in operation over a relatively long period, about two decades, was selected. The village was Sreebollobpur in Comilla-

Kotwali Thana, one of the first villages in which BARD undertook its development program in the early 1960s. Most components of BARD's program are found in Sreebollobpur. The village had an area of about 2.6 km² and a population of 1466 persons in October 1979. This had risen to 1507 persons by the end of the fieldwork in April 1981.

The most dramatic changes arising from the agricultural development programs in Sreebollobpur were economic. Area under mechanized irrigation (about 50% of cropped land) was higher than the national average, as were fertilizer application (80 and 50% of cropped area under HYVs and local varieties, respectively) and the use of pesticides (about 50 and 20% of cropped land under HYVs and local varieties, respectively). The presence of irrigation water and other supplementary inputs encouraged the adoption of HYVs. About 75% of the households adopted HYVs and over 50% of the cropped area was under HYVs. In contrast, only about 20% of the total cropped area devoted to paddy cultivation in the country was under HYVs in 1981–1982 (Bangladesh 1983:233). In addition, irrigation water and supplementary inputs facilitated the cultivation of the *boro* rice crop during the dry months (although its cultivation was limited to only about 12% of the cropped area in the country because irrigation water was lacking). The higher adoption of HYVs and the application of larger modern inputs have raised the per-unit-area demand for labour as well as raising yields. (Of the three varieties of rice grown in Bangladesh, *aus*, *aman*, and *boro*, the yield of *boro* is the highest [Bangladesh 1986].)

As a result of these improvements, the economic condition of the villagers was considerably better than that of the general population of rural Bangladesh. Other significant changes included greater labour force participation, changing occupational structure, higher levels of schooling, access to health facilities, and better communications. The crude labour-force participation rate was 44.5% for males and 35.0% for females, compared with 49.9 and 2.8% for males and females, respectively, in Bangladesh in 1981 (Bangladesh 1983:145). In a country where the vast majority is illiterate, the literacy level was surprisingly high — 85% for males and 61% for females. School attendance was also much higher in Sreebollobpur than elsewhere — 70% and about 50%, respectively, for males and females. The study village was exposed to some modern health facilities and modern ideas concerning hygiene and sanitation were being moderately accepted. A qualified aleopathic doctor and two homeopathic doctors lived in the village, as well as three traditional healers. In contrast to most villages of Bangladesh where the usual source of drinking water is a tank (reservoir) or pond, most inhabitants of Sreebollobpur used water from a tubewell for drinking. About 10% of the villagers used modern or semimodern latrines.

The villagers had reasonably good access to the media. There were 50 radios and 2 television sets in the community. Six persons received daily newspapers and these were read by about 15 persons. Radio, television, and newspapers often carried family-planning messages. Sreebollobpur was much better supplied with electricity than elsewhere in rural Bangladesh, where most villages are yet to be electrified: of 227 households in Sreebollobpur, 83 were supplied with electricity.

MARITAL STATUS AND AGE AT MARRIAGE

Marriage is almost universal in Bangladesh. In 1981, about 20% of females aged 15–19 years and about 1% of those older than 19 years were single in Bangladesh. The corresponding figures for males were 92 and 12%, respectively (Khuda 1982:table 1). The mean age at first marriage in Bangladesh, as in the rest of the subcontinent, has been low although it is slowly rising with time. In 1975–1976, the mean age at first marriage among all ever-married women in Bangladesh was 12.3 years (Bangladesh 1978:table 5.4). The mean age at first marriage among all ever-married women in the study village was 15.4 years, i.e., 3.1 years higher than that of Bangladeshi women in 1975–1976 (Table 1).

Mean age at first marriage among all ever-married women was highest among those now aged 20–24 years; it declined with a rise in present age. About 60% of women under 20 years of age were single, hence the low age at marriage shown applies only to a minority of women in this age group. When mean age at first marriage among ever-married women is examined by birth cohorts and current age, the rising age at marriage in Sreebollobpur over time shows even more clearly (Table 2). In general, the earlier the birth cohort, the lower was the age at first marriage and vice versa. A similar pattern was observed in Bangladesh as a whole (Bangladesh 1978:table 5.3). Because about 60% of women under 20 years of age were single and most of them belonged to the last birth cohort, age at marriage among women in the last birth cohort was slightly lower than those in the previous cohort.

Age at marriage was positively associated with schooling. Women with primary schooling and those with schooling beyond primary level were married, on the average, 2.2 and 3.7 years later, respectively, than those with no schooling. Attitude toward female age at marriage has been changing for some time. Some parents whose daughters were still studying said that they would like their daughters to be educated beyond secondary school, after which they would be married. Two of the village girls in their early 20s were studying at Dhaka University and their parents were reluctant to arrange their marriages until they had completed their education.

Table 1. Mean age of first marriage among ever-married women by their current age in Sreebollobpur.

Current age (years)	Mean age at first marriage (years)	Number of women
Below 20	15.2	38
20–24	17.3	50
25–29	17.1	54
30–34	16.7	31
35–39	15.7	31
40–44	15.0	29
45–49	13.4	27
Above 49	13.5	80
All ages	15.5	340

Table 2. Mean age at first marriage among ever-married women by birth cohort and present age in Sreebollobpur.

Birth cohort	Present age (years)		All ages	Number of women
	Below 30	Above 29		
Before 1925	–	12.3	12.3	59
1925–1934	–	14.8	14.8	48
1935–1944	–	15.4	15.4	60
1945–1954	17.1	16.7	16.9	85
After 1954	16.4	–	16.4	88

Age at marriage was also positively associated with landholding, a proxy for economic status. Women belonging to the landed households were married, on average, 1.5 years later than those belonging to landless households. The more prosperous were also relatively more educated, and age at marriage was positively related to education. Landholding, therefore, appears to affect age at marriage through its effects on education. Moreover, economic pressures faced by landless and land-poor households often compel them to arrange for early marriage of their daughters.

FAMILY PLANNING

Knowledge of family planning is almost universal in Bangladesh and 98% of the respondents in Sreebollobpur knew about contraceptives. The most commonly known methods in Sreebollobpur were "the pill," condoms, tubal ligation, vasectomy, and plastic coil. Respondents said they had first heard about family planning from the family-planning workers (30%) or over the radio (20%).

Over 70% of males in Sreebollobpur and about 50% of females supported contraception. This support was highest among males in their 30s and among females in their 20s. From the point of view of policy, this is encouraging as it indicates that the relatively younger couples may be appropriate "targets" for family-planning communication! The higher the educational level of the respondents, the higher was the proportion expressing their support for family planning.

In spite of widespread knowledge of and support for family planning, however, most couples in Bangladesh do not use it. Although family-planning practice has certainly increased over the past decade (Khuda 1984), only 35.7% of couples surveyed in 1981 had ever used contraception and only 18.6% were current users (Bangladesh 1981a, 1981b). In the study village, ever-use was 41% in 1980–1981 and current use was 25% (Table 3). The pill and condom were the two most widely used modern methods of contraception, accounting for 69% of current use of modern methods. In 1979, these two methods accounted for 57% of current use of modern methods in the country. The relatively higher proportion of couples using these two methods in Sreebollobpur than in Bangladesh in general perhaps reflects the longer history of the family-planning program in Sreebollobpur than in other areas.

Husband's and wife's education were positively related to contraceptive use in Sreebollobpur, as in Bangladesh in general (Bangladesh 1978,

Table 3. Distribution (%) of respondents in Sreebollobpur reporting ever-use and current use of family planning by method, 1980–1981.

Method	Ever-use	Current use
Modern		
Pill	12.7	3.7
Condom	6.0	3.7
Ligation	2.5	2.5
Plastic coil	1.7	0.5
Abortion	0.5	–
Foam	0.5	–
Vasectomy	0.3	0.3
All modern methods	24.2	10.7
Traditional		
Safe period	6.2	5.2
Withdrawal	11.0	9.3
All traditional methods	17.2	14.5
Total	41.4	25.2

1981a, 1981b, 1984). Previous use of contraception and size of landholding were also positively related in Sreebollobpur, although no systematic relationship was observed with respect to current use.

FERTILITY LEVELS AND DIFFERENTIALS

From estimates of age-specific fertility rates for Bangladesh (reported in various studies) and Sreebollobpur (Table 4), childbearing is highest among women aged 20–24 years and, although it remains high among women in the next two age groups (25–29 and 30–34 years), it tends to decline as age advances. In the study village, fertility was highest among women aged 15–19 years, indicating a strong urge on the part of newly married women to demonstrate their ability to have a child. Beyond 19 years of age, however, fertility in all other age groups in Sreebollobpur was considerably lower than in the other areas. Among women aged 35–39 years, fertility was only about half that reported elsewhere.

Another way of measuring fertility is to examine the mean number of children born to women who have been or are currently married (Table 5). Bangladeshi women achieve more than 50% of their completed fertility before reaching 30 years of age but they continue to bear children quite late into their reproductive life. A comparison with the data from the Bangladesh Fertility Survey of 1975–1976 shows that completed family size in the study village was lower than in Bangladesh as a whole. In fact, among all age groups except 15–19 years, the mean number of children born to women in Sreebollobpur was lower than in Bangladesh as a whole, especially among women aged 20–24 and 30–34 years.

The mean number of children born to ever-married women in the study village was inversely associated with their educational level (Table 6). Those who had not been to school had the highest fertility — 0.8 more children, on average, than those with primary schooling and 2.5 children more than those with at least secondary school. Because age at marriage is positively associated with education in Sreebollobpur, the lower fertility among the educated is at least partly due to their later marriage.

42

Table 4. Age-specific marital fertility rates and associated indicators of fertility in Bangladesh and Sreebollobpur.

| Age (years) | DSEP[a] 1960–1961 | BFS 1975–1976 | Other studies | | | | Sreebollobpur | |
			Barkait 1976	Matlab[b] 1979	Kotwali 1958–1959	Kotwali 1966–1967	Fertility rate 1979–1981	Currently married women
15–19	234	310	225	130	283	248	432	37
20–24	337	321	333	297	333	279	213	47
25–29	280	266	286	302	300	242	250	48
30–34	258	229	260	245	253	199	172	29
35–39	161	157	170	154	219	126	71	28
40–44	34	73	94	40	198	62	0	24
45–49	18	27	3C	9	–	–	0	19
TFR	6.6	6.3	7.0	5.9	8.5[c]	6.2[c]	4.5	
CBR	47.0	46.7	NA	35.0	NA	NA	30.7	

Sources: Stoeckel and Chowdhury 1973; Cain et al. 1976; Khan and Lewis 1976; Bangladesh 1978; Khuda 1978; Chowdhury et al. 1982; Miranda 1982; continuous recording of vital events from October 1979 to April 1981 in Sreebollobpur.

Abbreviations: BFS = Bangladesh Fertility Survey; TFR = Total fertility rate; CBR = Crude birth rate.

[a]Births per 1000 ever-married women.
[b]Age-specific fertility rate.
[c]Total marital fertility rate.

Table 5. Mean number of children born to ever-married women in Bangladesh and Sreebollobpur by their age.

Age (years)	Census 1961	Census 1974	DSEP 1961	BFS 1975–1976	Sreebollobpur (1979) Children (mean)	Sreebollobpur (1979) Women (number)
15–19	0.77	0.67	0.63	0.85	0.92	55
20–24	2.24	1.92	2.34	2.45	1.90	54
25–29	3.51	3.29	3.89	4.24	4.04	54
30–34	4.64	4.59	5.12	5.71	4.19	31
35–39	5.24	5.53	5.83	6.71	5.77	32
40–44	5.49	5.83	6.08	7.10	6.00	29
45–49	5.74	6.01	6.27	6.73	6.52	27

Sources: Khuda 1978; Miranda 1982; Sreebollobpur household census 1979.
Abbreviations: BFS = Bangladesh Fertility Survey.

Table 6. Mean number of children born to ever-married women by education, landholding, and current age in Sreebollobpur.

Characteristics	Current age (years) Below 30	Current age (years) Above 29	All ages	Number of women
Education				
No schooling	2.87	5.59	4.68	234
Primary schooling	2.29	5.47	3.90	71
Secondary schooling or more	1.46	5.00	2.17	35
All	2.45	5.55	4.26	340
Landholding (ha)				
Below 0.004	2.19	5.51	4.06	62
0.004–0.4	2.60	5.20	4.10	137
0.4–0.8	2.69	5.94	4.65	81
Above 0.8	2.08	5.83	4.27	60
All	2.45	5.55	4.26	340

Because mean age at first marriage among the women surveyed was 15.4 years, it is reasonable to use this age (approximately) as a dividing point to examine the effect of age at marriage on fertility. Thus, we grouped the women into two categories: those married before 16 years of age and those married later. The first group included 53% of women and they had an average of 1.6 children more than those in the second group.

The mean number of children born to ever-married women in the study village rises with an increase in the size of landholding but falls when landholding exceeds 0.8 ha, especially among the younger cohort. This relationship was not, however, statistically significant.

FERTILITY IDEALS AND ATTITUDES

Family size is generally believed to be influenced by the cultural ideals and attitudes of a population. Therefore, we investigated the attitudes and ideals of Sreebollobpur residents toward family size, son preference, and family planning.

The average number of children desired by males and females was virtually identical: 4.6 children for men and 4.5 for women. To determine the local attitude to family size, the respondents were asked to say what they considered to be "many" and "few" children. Males and females considered 5.2 and 6.3 children, respectively, to be "many" and 2.6 and 2.8, respectively, to be "few." On this basis, most respondents apparently felt that couples should have between 3 and 5 or 6 children.

Both males and females indicated a higher number of sons than daughters, a reflection of son preference. The number specified as "many" was higher among the relatively older respondents, and those who had not been to school, than among the younger respondents, and those who had been to school.

When asked "If a friend, relation, or neighbour decides to have only two children, would you consider this to be a wise decision?" about 60% of the respondents said "yes." By contrast, in a traditional Bangladeshi village, less than 50% of the respondents considered this a wise decision (Khuda 1977).

Over 50% of respondents (63% of males and 43% of females) would accept a theoretical situation in which, if offered some economic benefits (such as seeds, fertilizers, irrigation water, pesticides, etc.) free for 1 year, they would agree not to have children for the next 3 years. In the traditional village, only 10% agreed (Khuda 1977).

Over 50% of respondents — about 40% of males and over 65% of females — said that they would continue to have children until a son was born. This suggests that son preference is stronger among females than among males, perhaps because females are more dependent on their sons during old age and in times of stress, particularly when they become widows. However, the sizable proportion of respondents who said that they would not continue to have children until a son is born surely indicates a change in attitudes, because most people of Bangladesh, especially those in rural areas, are traditionally known to have strong son preference.

Surprisingly, 60% of the respondents perceived no advantages in having a large number of children. By contrast, only 25% of the respondents in the traditional village had the same perception (Khuda 1977:695). Economic pressure was perceived by 50% of the Sreebollopbur respondents to be the main disadvantage of having many children and over 80% of these said that their main economic problems stemmed from educational costs for children. In addition, it was almost universally agreed that girls are an economic burden to their families at the time of marriage.

Although many Sreebollobpur residents favoured a relatively large number of children, they did agree that some limits were needed. Many were aware of the economic pressures and hardships they are likely to face if they have more children than they can afford. Our in-depth interviews with various residents of Sreebollobpur revealed that their attitudes toward family size and family planning have been changing. The following selection of case studies is intended to represent different groups.

Respondent S.A.

S.A. is 36 years old, and works as an office assistant in Comilla Town. He has 0.3 ha of land, which he has sharecropped out to others. His two

45

sons (7 and 12 years old) and one daughter (10 years) are studying. He has been using family planning (condom) since his last child was born, and says he would not like to have any more children:

> Children are no more as cheap as they used to be in our times. Sons must receive proper education, if they are to get jobs in the formal sector, and daughters, if they are to get husbands. Children now demand more than they used to before. My neighbour has a radio, and my children have been urging me to buy one. I have finally bought one, but it would not have been possible if I had more children.

Respondent *A.K.*

A.K. is 48 years old. He is a farmer, owning 0.8 ha of land. Four of his five daughters and one of his two sons are married. The youngest son (aged 14) and youngest daughter (aged 11) go to school. His eldest son works on his farm, and he wants his youngest son to complete college education and get an urban job. Although he realizes the cost of educating his son, he maintains that it has to be done, saying, "For how long can agriculture continue to provide employment to the increasing number of people?"

He has seven grandchildren, and hopes that his children will do something to stop having more children than they can afford: "After all, children are becoming more expensive these days."

Respondent *A.M.*

A.M., a landless labourer, is 42 years old. Three of his four daughters are married. One of his sons (aged 18 years) is working as a day labourer; the other son (aged 10 years) is in school. His youngest daughter (aged 8 years) goes to a religious school. He and his son cannot find employment throughout the year, and their family income is just sufficient to meet the bare necessities of life. He is concerned about what will happen when his elder son gets married and moves away from home. He would like his youngest son to complete secondary school but he doubts whether he will be able to complete even primary school.

> We have been using family planning since the birth of our last child. We would have been better off if we had begun after the birth of our third or fourth child. If we had three or four children, it might have been possible to give secondary school education to one, or even two, but it is not possible now. If I were to start my marital life today, I would not have more than three or four children, even if they were all daughters.

Respondent *K.A.*

K.A., 65 years old, is a rich farmer, and owns 2.6 ha of land. Three of his four sons and his three daughters are married. Two of his daughters had no education, the third completed primary school. His eldest son had no education, his second and third sons had some secondary schooling, and his youngest son had a college education and is working in an office at Dhaka. *K.A.* would like his youngest son to get married to an educated girl and live in Dhaka.

> After all, I feel proud that my son has been living in Dhaka city. Why shouldn't he continue to live there when he is married? He should, of course, continue to maintain close links with us, and help us whenever we need his help.

K.A. has several grandchildren, and attaches great importance to their education. He says that children are more expensive these days because of the increased cost of schooling, and because they demand more things than in the past. He favours the idea of family planning: "Why should parents have more children than they can afford? I have told this to my children, and I hope they are wise. I consider two sons and one daughter the ideal number of children."

Respondent *S.Q.*

S.Q. is 25 years old, and has completed his secondary schooling. He owns 0.5 ha of land, and engages in part-time business. Last year, he married a woman of 18 years who had completed primary school. She is now pregnant. *S.Q.* would like to have a maximum of three children, and would be happy to have two sons and one daughter. If all three children are daughters, however, he will not have any more children. "If we have more children, we can neither bring them up properly nor afford to buy the material goods necessary to improve our standard of living."

DISCUSSION

The results of the study indicate that age at marriage and contraceptive use are higher, and fertility lower, in Sreebollobpur than in other parts of the country. These demographic changes could not have occurred without changes taking place in the society. It appears that economic improvements resulting from the agricultural development program were responsible for these changes.

With an increase in output and a better standard of living, people perceive a better future for themselves and for their children. They realize that their sons need education to obtain jobs in the formal sector and, hence, security and status. More parents are sending their daughters to school in the hopes of obtaining educated grooms for them. Schooling has raised the costs incurred for children.

Many rural families have acquired new tastes for modern consumer goods and services. The ownership of consumer durables such as radios, televisions, wristwatches, bicycles, motorcycles, chairs, and sewing machines was higher in Sreebollbpur than in other parts of Bangladesh, as was the per-household ownership and distribution of farm facilities such as ploughs, threshers, weeders, pesticide sprayers, and tubewells. These improved circumstances and the desire for continued improvement were "competitive" with the desire for more children, whose costs to parents were now more closely monitored.

The diversification of occupational structure also helps to lower fertility by reducing the value of child labour. Children belonging to nonfarm households do not contribute much labour, unlike children belonging to farm households. Those employed in the nonagricultural sector, particularly those in the formal service sector, want their children to undertake similar jobs when they grow up. Although wages in the urban sector may not be higher than rural earnings, nonagricultural employment does not depend on the seasons. Hence, many fathers still engaged in farming favoured the idea of at least one son taking up nonagricultural employment. Caldwell et al. (1982) observed a similar attitude among people in rural South India: formal sector employment entailed the rising costs of educating their children, particularly sons. Further, most of those working in the formal service sector employ outside labour or sharecrop out part of their land. Hence, their children do not contribute much labour to the family farm. Others employed in the service sector have no cultivable landholdings and their children do little productive work.

It has been noted earlier that levels of literacy and schooling were higher in the study village than the national figures. We also found that fertility was inversely related to the education of mothers. This is in line with findings from several other studies that show that education "depresses" fertility (Nag 1982). Education serves as an instrument of fertility decline by modernizing outlooks and attitudes, delaying the age at marriage, promoting contraception, and teaching hygiene, sanitation, and better health practices that lower infant mortality. Generally speaking, those who had been to school in Sreebollobpur wanted smaller families than those who had not been to school. A change in attitude toward the education of females was also evident, some parents deliberately delaying the marriages of their daughters until their education was completed. Such attitudes are likely to raise the female age at marriage further in future with consequent fertility-depressing effects.

COTTAGE INDUSTRY AND FERTILITY IN A VILLAGE IN WEST BENGAL, INDIA

Amit K. Bhattacharyya and Adrian C. Hayes[1]

This chapter analyzes the findings of a survey, conducted in 1980, of 327 households (embracing 362 families) in a rural area of West Bengal, India. The effects on fertility of participation by family members in a cottage industry producing costume jewelry are examined. This enterprise involved 25% of the families in the area in one way or another. Children began making these ornaments as early as 6 years of age and usually worked in the residence of an entrepreneur not far from their homes. Mothers working in the industry usually did so in their own homes, their employed children bringing work to them every day.

On the basis of preliminary survey results, participation in the cottage industry and fertility were clearly positively associated (Bhattacharyya 1982). Furthermore, children's participation in the industry was shown to be more strongly associated with fertility than mothers' participation. The mean number of live births for families where the wife was working in the industry was 4.3, compared with 3.9 where the wife was not working, a difference of less than 0.5. The mean number of live births for families where at least one child was working was 5.7, compared with 3.1 where no child was working, a difference of over 2.5. In our sample, mothers' participation in the industry appeared to have relatively little effect on fertility, presumably because mothers could work in their own homes and take care of their children at the same time. In this paper, therefore, the effect of children's participation on the mother's fertility is examined.

Although a positive association exists between the size of a family and its children's participation in the industry, it is not known whether this association is causal or spurious, and, if causal, in which direction the causation flows. Does children's participation in the industry motivate parents to have more children because the additional money income enhances or adds to other traditional values attached to children, or do some families that have a large number of children (for whatever reason) send some out to work to help make ends meet? In other words, "Is higher

[1] This paper was presented at the 52nd Annual Meeting of the Population Association of America, Pittsburgh, USA, 14–16 April 1983. The views expressed are those of the authors and do not necessarily represent the views of their institutions.

fertility a result of children's participation in cottage industry or is children's participation a result of higher fertility?"

DATA AND METHODS

The ideal research design for a study such as this would be a panel study that followed families through time, examining the history of their involvement in cottage industry and their fertility histories. In this way, one could determine whether there is anything distinctive about a family's fertility before it becomes involved in the industry or after it becomes employed. In particular, do families already have unusually high fertility when they first send children out to work, or does their fertility become unusually high after the children have begun work? In the ideal panel study, a sample of couples could be selected from specific age and marriage cohorts and followed through their work and fertility histories. To our knowledge, however, such a study has never been carried out and the data used here come from a single survey conducted by the author in 1980 in Howrah District of West Bengal in two phases.

First, a total household enumeration of 1044 households was conducted in an area where participation in the cottage industry was intensive. Information was collected on the household's participation in the ornament-making industry. For households participating in the industry, complete coverage was attempted. For those in which no one was working in the industry, every 10th household was sampled systematically. Multiple-family households having families with members working in the industry as well as families with no members working were included in the sample. In total, the sample contained 327 households and 362 families. The analysis here focuses on the 310 families in the sample with surviving children present.

Second, household heads were interviewed to collect information on the demographic, social, and economic characteristics of household members, as well as their participation in the industry. Two additional questionnaires, one for the husband and another for the wife, were administered to all "eligible couples" in each household. To be eligible, a couple must have been married once, be currently living together, and the wife must be 50 years of age or less. The husband's questionnaire contained detailed information on the economic value of children. The wife's questionnaire collected details concerning births and deaths of children, participation in the ornament-making industry, and current contraceptive status.

Hence, all households were given at least three questionnaires, plus separate ones for the husband and wife of each additional eligible couple in the family. The data allowed for the reconstruction, to some extent, of the history of each family's fertility and participation in the cottage industry. Questions were asked in the survey about fertility and the age at which any family member currently involved in the industry first joined it.

50

RESULTS

The children included in the data analysis in this paper are the children reported by mothers as alive at the time of the survey. Obviously, for analyzing the fertility *levels* of different couple types, data on children ever born would be preferable. We found, however, that mothers' reports on births of children who subsequently died were not reliable regarding the

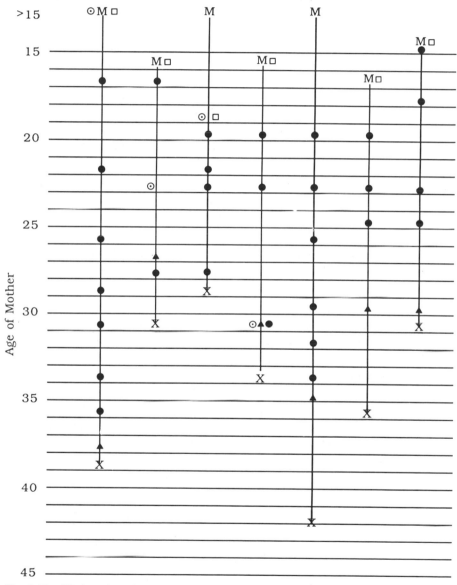

Fig. 1. Families' work and fertility histories: some cases of couples where the husband, wife, and at least one child are working in the industry based on wife's age (M, at marriage; X, at time of survey; •, at birth of child; □, when first participates in industry; ▲, when at least one child participates in industry; and ⊙, when husband first participates in industry).

51

timing of these births. Consequently, these data could not be used to calculate children ever born for different periods, i.e., before and after participation of the family in the industry. Therefore, the more reliable data on surviving children have been used to reconstruct a partial fertility history for each couple. Although we cannot estimate fertility levels precisely, we can use these data tentatively to check for fertility *differentials*, on the reasonable assumption that participation in the industry has no marked effect on a family's infant and child mortality.

The vertical axis in Fig. 1 represents the age of the mother. Each vertical line represents one mother in the sample: seven cases where husband, wife, and at least one child are participating in the industry are illustrated. The first woman, for example, was married before she was 15 years old, and is now 38. She had a child when she was 16 years old, another when she was 21, again when she was 25, 28, 30, 33, and 35 years old. She first participated in the industry before she was 15 years old; the second woman participated when she was 15 years, the third when she was 18 years.

Reconstructing families' work and fertility histories in this way with the mother as the point of reference enables us to determine the timing of two important events in each woman's reproductive history: the age at which she first participates in the industry and the age at which her children first participate in the industry. We can then compare the fertility of women before or after these events with the fertility of women from the same age or marriage cohort who do not share these events.

The mean number of surviving children of 310 eligible couples varies from 2.7 to 4.5 children per couple by "couple type" with a total sample mean of 3.5 (Table 1). If we aggregate some categories, we find that for cases where at least one child is working, the mean is 4.3; where the mother or at least one child, or both, are working, the mean is 3.8; where the mother is working but no child, it is 3.1; and where neither the mother nor child is working, the mean number of surviving children is 2.7.

Mothers with at least one working child have a greater number of living children than those in the same age category with no children participating, and the difference is more pronounced among older women (Table 2).

Young women participating have a higher than average number of living children (Table 3), but the differential disappears among women currently in their 30s and, among women now in their 40s, the difference is

Table 1. Number of families and surviving children by couple type.

Couple type[a]	Families	Children	Mean parity
I (H+ W+ C+)	29	111	3.8
II (H+ W+ C−)	37	106	2.9
III (H+ W− C+)	9	39	4.3
IV (H+ W− C−)	41	113	2.8
V (H− W+ C+)	49	221	4.5
VI (H− W+ C−)	51	164	3.2
VII (H− W− C+)	52	227	4.4
VIII (H− W− C−)	42	112	2.7
Total	310		

[a]H = husband; W = wife; C = child; + = working in industry; and − = not working in industry.

Table 2. Mean number of surviving children by participation of children and age of mother.

Age of mother (years)	At least one child participating in industry		No child participating in industry	
	Children (mean)	Mothers (number)	Children (mean)	Mothers (number)
20–24	–	0	1.7	43
25–29	3.8	10	3.2	43
30–34	3.6	25	3.3	47
35–39	4.7	33	3.8	14
40–49	4.9	71	3.8	24
Total		139		171

Table 3. Mean number of surviving children by participation and age of mother.

Age of mother (years)	Mean number of surviving children for mothers[a]	
	Participating	Nonparticipating
20–24	2.0	1.4
25–29	3.6	2.8
30–34	3.4	3.4
35–39	4.4	4.2
40–49	3.6	4.2

[a]166 participating and 144 nonparticipating mothers.

Table 4. Mean number of surviving children to a mother before and after at least one of her children starts working.

Current age of mother (years)	Mothers with at least one child participating				Mothers with no child participating	
	Mean number of children					
	Before participation	After participation	Total	Mothers	Mean number of children	Mothers
20–24	–	–	–	0	1.65	43
25–29	3.60	0.10	3.70	10	3.19	43
30–34	3.32	0.24	3.56	25	3.26	47
35–39	4.27	0.39	4.66	33	3.79	14
40–44	4.54	0.34	4.88	35	3.78	13
45–49	4.70	0.20	4.90	36	3.73	11

reversed, with those participating in the industry having a lower average number of surviving children.

If the number of surviving children of mothers with at least one child working is disaggregated into those living before any start working and those born and surviving thereafter, for women in all age categories, over 90% of their now-surviving children were born before any of their children started working (Table 4).

The births (of surviving children) per woman per year at risk were calculated by age category (Table 5). For example, women who are currently 25–29 years of age and have at least one child working, had an average of 0.30 births/year since they turned 25 before any of their children started working, and 0.06 births/year since they turned 25 after at least one of their children started working. Families with children working are characterized by a considerably higher fertility rate before the children start working than those families with no children working.

53

Table 5. Estimated births of currently surviving children per woman per year before and after at least one of her children starts working.

| Current age of mother (years) | Mothers with at least one child participating | | | Mothers with no child participating | |
| | Mean number of births | | | | |
	Before participation	After participation	Mothers	Mean number of births	Mothers
25–29	0.30	0.06	10	0.18	43
30–34	0.26	0.04	23	0.12	47
35–39	0.15	0.04	33	0.04	14
40–44	0.15	0.03	35	0.02	9

Table 6. Distribution (%) of the fathers' responses to the question "Do children earn more or less than the expenses incurred?" by work status of their children.

| Response | Working children in family | | |
	None	One	Most
Earns more than expenses	10	15	19
Earns as much as expenses	22	30	35
Earns less than expenses	68	53	40
Do not know	0	2	6
Total	100	100	100
Number	197	71	60

For families with children working, fertility declines dramatically when the children start work; furthermore, the fertility of these families, after participation starts, is as low as, or even lower than, it is for families with no children working.

The births reported in Table 5 are based on very small numbers of women in most instances. Furthermore, the reconstructions of families' work and fertility histories are only approximate. Nevertheless, the four points that emerge from this analysis are sufficiently consistent to merit attention:

- Families with children working in the cottage industry were larger than those without — roughly 30% larger in the case of those families in which the mother had nearly completed her fertile period.
- Families with working children were already relatively large when the children first participated in the cottage industry.
- Families with children working had completed over 90% of their cumulative fertility by the time their children started working.
- Families with working children appear to have fertility as low as, or even lower than, families with no children working, *after* the children started working.

In other words, children's participation in the cottage industry appears to cause a subsequent decline in fertility. High fertility may cause children's participation, but then the children's participation appears to act as a brake on additional fertility. It certainly does not increase fertility further.

The present survey also collected attitudinal data on how children's work was viewed by their parents. When fathers were asked if their

54

Table 7. Distribution (%) of the fathers' responses to the statement "The value of the work done by small children for their parents is more than the cost of the food they eat" by work status of their children.

Response	Working children in family		
	None	One	Most
Agree	12	14	17
Disagree	84	82	75
No opinion	4	4	8
Total	100	100	100
Number	197	71	60

Table 8. Distribution (%) of the fathers' responses to the statement "The best investment is in the education of our children" by work status of their children.

Response	Working children in family		
	None	One	Most
Agree	96	94	100
Disagree	3	6	0
No opinion	1	0	0
Total	100	100	100
Number	197	71	60

Table 9. Distribution (%) of the fathers' responses to the statement "The more children a man has, the poorer he becomes" by work status of their children.

Response	Working children in family		
	None	One	Most
Agree	84	92	85
Disagree	6	7	10
No opinion	10	1	5
Total	100	100	100
Number	197	71	60

children earned more or less than the expenses incurred and whether the value of the work done by small children for their parents is more than the cost of the food they eat, most responded "Earns less than expenses" (Table 6) and did not agree that the value of work done by small children is more than the cost of the food they eat (Table 7). Most significant is the fact that the modal response in either case does not vary with the work status of their children.

Fathers seem to believe that, in the short-run at least, the wealth flow from parents to children outweighs the wealth flow from children to parents. At the same time, this opinion is less common among fathers with children working in the industry. In Table 6, for example, 32% of fathers with no children working say that children earn more or as much as expenses incurred; for fathers with most of their children working, this figure is up to 54%. The income brought in by working children is, therefore, seen as significant by many of their fathers.

Yet, these same fathers (with most of their children working) are unanimous in their agreement with the statement that "The best investment is in the education of our children" (Table 8) and these fathers are just as likely to agree with the statement that "The more children a man has, the poorer he becomes" as fathers with no children working (Table 9). These attitudinal data suggest that fathers with working children may be as highly committed to the value of education, and perhaps other modern fertility values, as those with children not working but going to school; and that fathers with working children often recognize the economic value of children and the practical help this provides to the family. These two findings are consistent with our hypothesis that changes toward smaller family size values may occur at the same time as sending children out to work, and that the latter event might even prompt the former changes.

DISCUSSION

The population described here is not sufficiently large to provide any definitive answers concerning the relationship between fertility and the economic contributions of children. The following, however, is offered as an "interpretive sketch" of the findings, in the light of recent rethinking of demographic transition theory (Caldwell 1976; Easterlin 1980), especially those dimensions seeking to isolate the different economic, social, and cultural factors that determine the timing of fertility decline (Caldwell 1980).

With the advance of socioeconomic development in this rural area, children are enrolled in school. The value of children perceived by parents increases as they consider the long-term benefits that this education might bring in terms of future economic opportunities. At this stage, development may be said to have pronatalist, or at least not antinatalist, implications. All too soon, however, families living close to subsistence levels experience the costs of having a large number of children in school. To survive, they are compelled to take some of their children out of school and put them to work. In West Bengal today, where the ideal situation is to have a large number of offspring and to have them all in school, such a decision is made reluctantly, and is invariably accompanied by a sense of shame. The present study found that having to take children out of school and send them to work was generally viewed as somewhat of a family tragedy. Parents having to respond to economic pressures in this way are likely to perceive the short-term costs of having children, and to reduce their fertility after this point.

In other words, when the family has to send some children to work, a turning point has been reached. Before this threshold, the gradual assimilation of "modern" attitudes toward education is consistent with continued high fertility but, after this point, parents reconsider the value of children. Any further assimilation of modern values on their part is likely to be consistent with a desire to limit fertility. Therefore, taking children out of school and sending them to work seems to operate as an important threshold in a family's fertility behaviour.

In the present study, income-generating activities went hand in hand with distinct deterioration in the quality of life of the children who were taken away from school and sent to work. Interestingly, the countries of the Third World are increasingly encouraging the expansion of cottage and agroindustries to hasten economic development for the rural population. Our study highlights the kind of social forces these activities can generate and the demographic implications that may result. More studies are, therefore, needed to understand more fully the nature and variety of rural development activities currently underway in Third World nations and their implications for social and demographic change.

Agricultural and Sociodemographic Interrelationships: A Study of Three Areas at Different Levels of Development in Tolima, Colombia

Diego Giraldo Samper

The most significant aspect of the Colombian population over the last 50 years has been the declining rate of population increase. This change is closely linked with the social and economic transformations that have followed one upon the other as the country, as a whole, has developed. This chapter discusses the dynamics of population growth in the context of specific socioeconomic conditions, focusing particularly on their relation to production.

Studies in recent years on the agrarian structure of Colombia distinguished three agricultural systems that can be identified by their production factors and product destination. The first is in the modern capitalist sector where land, capital, and wage labour are used intensively to produce large volume at a high rate of productivity, mostly to supply raw material to the industrial market. This expands the agricultural market.

The opposite system, the smallholding sector, makes intensive use of land but minimal use of capital. Precapitalist tenant relationships with landlords still survive in some cases, and the contribution of unpaid family labour is important. This system consists of groups of small production units (*minifundia*, smallholdings) or large but unproductive units where capitalist relationships have not been developed (*latifundia*).

Between these two systems are production units of a transitional nature that have not yet developed their production methods to an advanced level. Although this type of unit does not have capital resources to invest in production, it does depend upon wage labour functioning at a high rate of productivity, generally focusing on one crop oriented toward outside markets. Such units that, in Colombia, typically produce coffee represent a traditional form of capitalism and, historically speaking, served to link Colombian production with foreign markets. It was also through them that internal trade developed.

Theoretical Considerations

In units of the modern capitalist type, the predominant production relationships determine the roles of families and their income, allowing one or more members of the household to participate in the wage labour force. Consequently, the receipt of a salary is a major determinant of a family's economic and demographic behaviour and organization. It is in search of a salary and adequate means of subsistence that women and children join the work force, either full or part time. This certainly affects the standards and values by which they regulate their demographic behaviour with regard to marriage and divorce, types of marriage, number of children, decisions about and opportunities for migration, and even morbidity and mortality.

Smallholding units are distinguished by the almost exclusive participation of their members in family labour. Only occasionally does a member of the family leave and take up wage labour. Families assign tasks to each member in the production unit, ensuring the maintenance and subsistence of the family unit. Quite logically, one would expect their demographic behaviour to adapt to prevailing production requirements. Smallholding families could be expected to have a stable and relatively numerous family group, obedient to the unilateral decisions of the household head about the role of each member of the family in the domestic economy.

The traditional units of capitalist production, which have not yet modernized, are distinguished by the predominance of wage labour that accompanies the concentration of landholdings in large estates such as coffee plantations. This process has resulted in the formation of a specialized labour market in the coffee-growing sector. Occasionally, although never as the dominant form, one encounters sharecropping or other arrangements.

The demand for wage labour and family participation in productive labour depend, to a great extent, upon the area of land owned. In those small operations that still survive, the household head (usually the man) looks after the farm but also does wage labour on a part-time basis. Spouses (usually the woman) play an important role in the production of coffee, as well as in harvesting ancilliary crops. In the larger units, as well as family labour, a large number of day workers are hired according to seasonal requirements.

In more concrete terms, our analysis has been structured with the following hypotheses in mind with respect to the relationship between productive structure, family organization, and demographic behaviour.

First, in modern capitalist units of production, wage labour predominates and determines, to a large extent, family survival strategies. Family strategies depend on opportunities for salaried work for however many family members need it to subsist, and hence on the demand and supply of labour. The need to earn a salary from available sources may also result in migration within and between regions. Previous studies have shown that families in the modern capitalist sector are taking up fundamentally urban and modern ways of life. Their demographic behaviour, therefore, will comprise both migration and a tendency toward lower fertility.

Second, production units of the smallholding type are based on activities that permit the family to subsist upon the produce obtained from their land. The work capacities of the various members are fundamental to the social and economic organization of the family, although other factors such as the quality and area of land, prices of produce, how surplus is marketed, and climatic conditions also must be taken into account. Nondomestic activities, which include sporadic wage labour by the household head, work by spouses in poorly paid tertiary activities, or departure of children, also affect the survival strategies of these families. Because production centres around family work, people tend to settle on their plots rather than migrate elsewhere. Migration usually involves children who are an excessive burden upon the productive capacities of the land and tends to be mainly intraregional.

Third, in production units of the traditional capitalist type, wage labour predominates. These units cannot be equated with modern ones, however, because their production is managed by the household head in the dual role of worker and boss and depends to a great extent upon the size of the unit. Size determines the specific activities of each member of the family at each stage of production. The specialization of productive activities also influences spatial mobility between regions of similar type. The most common form of migration is seasonal, to other coffee-growing regions. Family behaviour is, however, rural in style, although less so than that of the smallholdings. The level of fertility will still be high, therefore, and the massive displacement of population will be less evident than in the modern capitalist sector.

Scope of Study

The area selected for the study was a group of municipalities in the Department of Tolima. Families were selected as the basic units of study according to their productive organization within the capitalist economy, ranging from the most traditional forms to more modern types of agricultural and industrial production.

A stratified sample of 494 families, representative of the entire zone, was selected and interviewed in August–September 1982. Of these, 24 interviews had to be discarded because of inconsistencies, providing a total number of 470 completed interviews.

Results

The smallholding sector contained 43.2% of the families; the modern capitalist sector, 30.6%; and the traditional capitalist sector, 26.2%. Chaparral was the largest and most populous municipality (Table 1).

Table 1. Distribution of population and families by municipality of residence and productive sector.

Municipality	Smallholding sector				Traditional capitalist sector				Modern capitalist sector			
	Population		Families		Population		Families		Population		Families	
	Number	%	Number	%	Number	%	Number	%	Number	%	Number	%
Guamo	292	18.7	35	17.3	197	24.9	35	28.5	261	28.7	41	28.5
Purificación	240	15.4	30	14.8	65	8.2	9	7.3	268	29.5	38	26.4
Saldana	227	14.5	22	10.8	52	6.6	6	4.9	93	10.2	16	11.1
Chaparral	804	51.4	116	57.1	478	60.3	73	59.3	288	31.6	49	34.0
Total	1563	100.0	203	100.0	792	100.0	123	100.0	910	100.0	144	100.0

Table 2. Characteristics of productive sectors sampled.

Characteristic	Smallholding	Traditional capitalist	Modern capitalist
Position of household head	Proprietor of small or medium holding[a] Salaried Shareholder or lessee	Proprietor of small, medium, or large holding Salaried Shareholder or lessee (10+ ha)	Proprietor of small, medium, or large holding Salaried Shareholder or lessee (10+ ha)
Principal crop produced	Cotton Sugar Sorghum	Coffee	Food crops
Destination of produce	Principally or exclusively household consumption Small surpluses to market	Principally urban markets Small proportion dedicated to family consumption	Exclusively urban markets
Size of farm where household head works	Very small Small Medium	Small Medium Large	Small Medium Large
Type of labour used	Proprietor Proprietor with unpaid family labour Shareholder or lessee Shareholder or lessee with unpaid nonfamily labour	Salaried agricultural workers Proprietors and seasonal salaried agricultural workers Proprietors, seasonal salaried agricultural workers, and family labour Shareholder or lessee with salaried agricultural workers, permanent or seasonal labour, and paid family labour	Salaried agricultural workers Proprietors and salaried agricultural workers Shareholder or lessee with salaried agricultural workers

[a]Holdings were classified as very small (0–5 ha), small (5–10 ha), medium (10–100 ha), and large (over 100 ha).

DEMOGRAPHIC CHARACTERISTICS

In most sectors, men outnumbered women, males constituting 53.7% in the traditional capitalist sector and 49.7% in the modern. The gap is particularly wide in the municipalities of Guamo (54.3% male) and Saldana (59.6% male), indicating a greater tendency for women to migrate.

In the smallholding and modern capitalist sectors, 47.9% of the population were under the age of 15, as were 45.3% in the traditional sector. Of special interest was the high proportion of children (nearly 20%) in the smallholding sector, compared with 18.0% in the modern capitalist sector, and 14.6% in the traditional capitalist sector. These proportions are consistent with evidence on fertility differentials among the three groups.

ECONOMIC CHARACTERISTICS

Selected social and economic characteristics of the sample population are presented in Tables 2 and 3 by sector. In the smallholding sector, families depended upon the exploitation of their small farms and did not seek wage employment. Most families owned their land or farmed in partnership or rental arrangements. This required the assistance of spouses and some of the children. Occupational diversification was minimal: almost 20% of peasant families depended entirely on what they produced on their plots and received no cash payment for the work they did. Sometimes, however, the family economy expanded beyond these limits because of contributions received from children or relatives not living at home. Unemployment severely affected these families; consequently, income was the lowest of the three sectors.

The traditional capitalist sector, perhaps the most heterogeneous in its composition, consisted of family groups engaged mainly in the cultivation of coffee, although generally in association with other crops that provided shade and food for family consumption. The families classified

Table 3. Social and economic characteristics of population by sector (% distribution).

	Smallholding		Traditional capitalist		Modern capitalist	
	%	Number	%	Number	%	Number
Distribution by age group (years)						
0–14	48.3	748	45.3	359	47.7	434
15–44	40.9	634	39.1	310	41.5	378
45–64	9.4	146	12.5	99	9.2	84
Above 64	0.6	10	2.1	17	1.2	11
No response	0.8	12	0.9	7	0.3	3
Land tenure of household head						
Proprietor	70.9	144	52.8	65	29.2	42
Sharecropper/lessee	25.6	52	24.4	30	6.9	10
Salaried labourer	–	0	17.1	21	59.7	86
Domestic labourer	2.0	4	5.7	7	–	0
No response	1.5	3	–	0	4.2	6

(continued)

63

Table 3. Concluded.

	Smallholding		Traditional capitalist		Modern capitalist	
	%	Number	%	Number	%	Number
Remuneration of household head						
Salary	77.8	158	91.9	113	93.4	134
No salary	19.2	39	5.7	7	4.1	6
No response	3.0	6	2.4	3	2.5	4
Remuneration of spouse						
Salary	6.9	14	1.6	2	27.1	39
No salary	86.7	176	91.1	112	72.2	104
No response	6.4	13	7.3	9	0.7	1
Unemployment						
Household heads	11.3	23	6.5	8	8.3	12
Spouses	3.9	8	1.6	2	3.5	5
Children	5.4	11	1.6	2	6.2	9
Monthly income of household head (COP)[a]						
3500–7000	10.8	22	1.6	2	18.0	26
7001–10000	37.0	75	26.0	32	31.2	45
10001–15000	30.5	62	22.8	28	11.8	17
15001–20000	10.8	22	14.6	18	12.5	18
Above 20000	8.9	18	22.8	28	9.8	14
No response	2.0	4	12.2	15	16.7	24
Type of labour used[b]						
Salaried nonfamily	10.2	20	84.2	80	92.3	48
Family	72.4	142	51.0	49	42.3	22
Occupation of household head						
Farming	74.4	151	82.9	102	83.3	120
Household services	8.9	18	4.9	6	3.4	5
Construction	3.9	8	1.6	2	4.9	7
Other services	5.9	12	2.4	3	2.8	4
Housework	2.5	5	5.7	7	0.7	1
Disabled or ill	–	0	0.8	1	1.4	2
No occupation	2.9	6	1.7	2	2.8	4
No response	1.5	3	–	0	0.7	1
Occupation of spouse[c]						
Farming	4.9	10	0.8	1	20.8	30
Household services	–	0	–	0	8.3	12
Housework	84.7	172	91.1	112	62.5	90
Domestic vending	3.9	8	0.8	1	0.7	1
Handicrafts	5.9	12	–	0	0.7	1
Other services	0.5	1	0.8	1	6.2	9
No occupation	–	0	6.5	8	0.7	1
Household only	76.8	156	81.3	100	60.4	87
Housework and other work	16.7	34	11.4	14	25.7	37
Only other work	0.5	1	0.8	1	12.5	18
Not applicable	5.9	12	6.5	8	1.4	2
Distribution by monthly family income (COP)						
3500–7000	6.9	14	1.6	2	13.9	20
7001–10000	40.4	82	24.4	30	33.3	48
10001–15000	32.5	66	24.4	30	16.6	24
15001–20000	11.3	23	14.6	18	11.1	16
20001–30000	7.9	16	14.6	18	5.6	8
Above 30000	1.0	2	8.2	10	5.6	8
No income/No response	–	0	12.2	15	13.9	20

[a]Minimum rural wages in 1982: 7020 Colombian pesos (COP) = 108 U.S. dollars (USD).

[b]Percentages do not add to 100 because no extra labour may be used or both nonfamily and family labour may be used.

[c]Percentages do not add to 100 because spouse may have more than one occupation.

as middle producers formed a large proportion of this sector. Workers usually lived in nuclear families and, as one would expect, salaried workers were hired less frequently than in the modern capitalist sector. By far, the greater number of household heads were paid for their work, both from the sale of produce in local markets and from the sale of their labour. The participation of women in farming and animal husbandry was the highest of the three sectors, although, for the most part, it was not paid. This sector had the lowest rate of unemployment, both of household heads and of other members. Although family labour played a smaller role than in the smallholding sector, it was still used by 50% of landowning, leasing, or share-cropping families. A higher proportion of such labour was paid, particularly in the case of the medium landowners.

In the modern capitalist sector, in which agricultural labour predominated, 72.9% of the families were nuclear in structure. Almost 60% of families depended totally upon the work of the household head. The high proportion of day labourers made this sector the most vulnerable to unemployment, which affected a higher number of household heads than in the other sectors. In this sector, however, more paid labour was performed by women and children. Proprietors and lessees employed less family labour than in the other sectors, but when they did, they paid cash wages.

Occupationally, the population was engaged primarily in agriculture and animal husbandry. Thus, whereas in the smallholding sector 74.3% of the household heads were engaged primarily in agricultural labour, including animal husbandry and fishing, this increased to 82.9% in the traditional sector and 83.3% in the modern capitalist sector. These proportions were no doubt influenced by the timing of the interviews. For example, inquiries were done in the traditional sector at the time of the coffee harvest. On the other hand, the figure for the modern capitalist sector may represent an underestimate because interviewing took place during the slack agricultural period when land maintenance (mainly aerial spraying) was underway.

In the smallholding sector, one encountered the highest number of household heads engaged in activities not strictly connected with farming. Some worked in estate management, household services (including peddling), and personal services; others as security guards, porters, tire fitters, carpenters' assistants, and so on. In the traditional and modern capitalist sectors, the proportion engaged in such activities dropped by almost 50%. Paradoxically, although smallholding peasants are more closely bound to the land than owners or sharecroppers, their inability to find security for themselves and their families through cultivation drives them into a variety of dissimilar activities. Moreover, of household heads in the smallholding sector who worked in farming, almost 20% received no cash payment for their work. In the traditional and modern sectors, this proportion dropped to 5.7 and 4.1%, respectively. In the modern capitalist sector, this latter figure applied only to those household heads who had no occupation and those who reported domestic labour as their principal activity.

Women were involved in productive labour in different ways. In the smallholding sector, 84.7% of women worked exclusively in their homes; in the traditional capitalist sector, 91.0%; and in the modern capitalist,

62.5%. In this latter sector, many more were engaged in other activities such as farming, administrative and office work, sewing, and teaching. In the smallholding sector, handicrafts employed 5.9% of the women, mainly hatmaking and peddling small household articles. At first, women in this sector did not list their participation in farm work as an activity. When asked what else they did, however, the 84.7% of smallholders who listed housework as their only activity was reduced to 76.8%. In the traditional capitalist sector, the percentage dropped from 91.0 to 81.3%. In the modern capitalist sector, there was a smaller drop, from 62.5 to 60.4%.

Unemployment had an impact upon the incomes received in each sector. Surprisingly, it was not in the modern capitalist sector that the highest family incomes were found. In it, 18.1% of household heads earned incomes below the monthly minimum wage, and 20.8% of household heads had no income. In the smallholding sector, 20.8% of household heads earned less than the minimum wage, compared to only 1.6% in the traditional capitalist sector.

If one considers total family income, ascertained by questioning wives, children, and relatives who contributed to family subsistence, the following situation emerges. The contribution of family members to the household economy was most apparent in families with an income above minimum wage in all three sectors, particularly in families with an income above COP 10 000 (in 1982, 65 Colombian pesos [COP] = 1 U.S. dollar [USD]). This indicated that cash contributions by other members of the family were more common as family income rose. In the lowest income groups, there was less sharing of earning activities, especially by women and children.

Among the smallest landowners in the smallholding sector, wages were generally not paid to family workers. As the area of land owned increased, payments to family members, as well as to outside labourers, also increased. Thus, salaried workers were found on 83.3% of the farms in the middle-size group. The proportion of family workers was 41.7%, of whom 60% were paid. In the leasing and sharecropping families, however, employment of family members was even more widespread: 88.4% of the farms in this sector used family members to work the land. Of these, only 25.0% received any pay and only 13.5% of the farms in the group employed outside salaried labour.

In the traditional capitalist sector, family labour was also important among the small groups of smallholders, lessees, and sharecroppers. Over 75% of the households in this group employed family labour. Among the smallholders, about 33.3% paid their family members whereas, among the lessees and sharecroppers, 65.4% of the family members were paid for their work. In the group of medium landowners in the smallholding sector, 92.7% of farms hired outside labour. Pay to family members was also more prevalent: 82.3% paid wages to employed family members. The two large landholders in the sector employed no family members.

Among all groups in the capitalist sector, there was a high rate of wage labour, above 80% in all cases. However, among the small landowners, lessees, and sharecroppers, family workers were commonly employed and paid for their work. Wages were about 10% lower than those paid to nonfamily labour.

RELATIONSHIP BETWEEN DEMOGRAPHIC AND ECONOMIC CHARACTERISTICS

The largest households (including both family and nonfamily members) were found in the smallholding sector (Table 4), where family members numbered 7.7 on average. In the traditional and modern capitalist sectors, family size dropped to 6.4 and 6.3, respectively. This indicates the existence of differing fertility behaviour in the three sectors. Smallholding families had an average of 5.2 live-born children, compared with 3.8 children in the other two sectors (Table 5). Income was also related to family size in this sector (Table 6). Except for those earning less than the minimum salary, there was a clear tendency toward a smaller average number of children as size of landholding and income increased: from 5.73 children per family in the income range COP 7001–10 000 to around 4 children in families with an income above COP 20 000. Average family size was also higher among sharecroppers and lessees (5.81 children) than among middle-sized landowners (4.42 children).

In the traditional capitalist sector, the tendency was similar, but not consistently linear. Although the average family size was highest in families earning less than COP 7000, this applied to only two families. In the income group COP 7000–15 000, however, the average number of children was above 4, and it fluctuated between 3.2 and 3.7 above that income level. As in the smallholding sector, those families in share-cropping and leasing systems had an average of 4.67 children, compared to 3.29 children for medium landholders.

The modern capitalist sector does not show any consistent pattern by income or size of landholding (Tables 5 and 6), but this may be due to the small number of families in some categories. Medium-sized landowners in the sector had the lowest average number of children (3.6), compared with 4.73 for the small landowners. The figure for the large landowners cannot be taken as indicative because there was only one such family.

Marriage patterns were also compared across the three sectors with respect to the age at which women began to live with men, the number of unions, and their duration. In all three sectors, the age of the women contracting unions was lower than in previous generations. The greatest drop in the age of women entering unions was in the capitalist sectors: these women now enter a union 2.4 years younger compared with 30 or more years ago. Among smallholders, the drop is 1.5 years. Whereas one might have expected that, in the smallholding sector, women would get married earlier than in the others, quite the opposite appeared. The earliest age of marriage was in the modern capitalist sector. Hence, contrary to most studies that find increasing delays in age of marriage as a society modernizes, there does not appear to be this link in the area studied. In fact, the age of marriage was younger in the most-developed productive sectors.

Information was also obtained on the ideal number of children families would have. For the most part, women gave responses similar to the average number they already had. When asked whether families found their children economically valuable, 38% of families in the smallholding

Table 4. Size of households by sector.[a]

Size (number of members)	Smallholding sector				Traditional capitalist sector				Modern capitalist sector			
	Families		Members		Families		Members		Families		Members	
	Number	%	Number	%	Number	%	Number	%	Number	%	Number	%
2	6	3.0	12	0.8	2	1.4	4	0.4	0	–	0	–
3	2	1.0	6	0.4	12	8.3	36	4.0	10	8.1	30	3.8
4	5	2.5	20	1.3	18	12.5	72	7.9	17	13.8	68	8.6
5	18	8.9	90	5.7	27	18.8	135	14.8	21	17.1	105	13.3
6	33	16.3	198	12.7	27	18.8	162	17.8	22	17.9	132	16.7
7	37	18.2	259	16.6	17	11.8	119	13.1	21	17.1	147	18.5
8	35	17.2	280	17.9	17	11.8	136	15.0	9	7.3	72	9.1
9	24	11.8	216	13.8	10	6.9	90	9.9	8	6.5	72	9.1
Above 9	43	21.1	482	30.8	14	9.7	156	17.1	15	12.2	166	20.9

[a]Includes family members who are not present as well as those present, i.e., total family size.

Table 5. Average number of children ever-born by size of landholding and sector.

Size of landholding	Smallholding sector		Traditional capitalist		Modern capitalist	
	Children	Families	Children	Families	Children	Families
Minifundia	5.17	84	–	0	–	0
Small landowners	4.67	48	4.50	8	4.73	11
Medium landowners	4.42	12	3.29	55	3.60	30
Large landowners	–	0	3.50	2	4.00	1
Sharecroppers and lessees	5.81	52	4.67	30	2.80	10

Table 6. Average number of children ever-born by monthly family income and sector.

Income groups (COP)[a]	Smallholding sector		Traditional capitalist		Modern capitalist	
	Children	Families	Children	Families	Children	Families
3500–7000	2.57	14	6.00	2	4.85	20
7001–10000	5.73	82	4.40	30	3.08	48
10001–15000	5.34	67	4.47	30	3.92	24
15001–20000	4.70	23	3.22	18	4.13	16
20001–30000	4.31	16	3.50	18	4.00	8
Above 30000	4.00	2	3.70	10	3.50	8
No response	–	0	–	9		20

[a]In 1982, 65 Colombian pesos (COP) = 1 U.S. dollar (USD).

sector said that children helped with the work, compared with only 19 and 13% in the traditional and modern capitalist sectors, respectively. In these latter sectors, however, children were seen more as a source of support in old age than in the smallholding sector. In the modern sector, more than 25% of families considered the cost of maintaining children a problem whereas, in the traditional and smallholding sectors, only 13 and 18% of families, respectively, considered offspring a financial burden.

The knowledge and use of contraceptives was also investigated in the three sectors. In the smallholding sector, almost 20% of the women knew nothing about family planning. In the capitalist sectors, the proportion dropped to less than 15%. The use of birth-control methods was most common in the modern and traditional capitalist sectors. At the time of the inquiry, they were used by over 55% of the women in these sectors and by 43% of those in the smallholding sector. Important differences appeared with respect to when women began to use birth control. In the modern capitalist sector, 43% of women who used birth control did so after the birth of their second child; in the smallholding sector, only 28% did so at this point; and in the traditional sector, 27%. Most of the women in the smallholding and traditional sectors who used birth-control methods did so only after the birth of their fourth child, and a large percentage (26% in the smallholding sector, 24% in the traditional capitalist sector, and 7% in the modern sector) did not begin to use them until they had borne as many as eight children.

Various questions in the interview were designed to determine the number of migrants per family, the type of migratory flow, and the time involved. To measure seasonal migration, which is significant in the study zone, all movements outside the municipality of one's birth by any member of a family for at least 1 month were counted. There were migrants (29% of the population) in 58% of families in the modern capitalist sector, and in 54% of families in the traditional sector, where there were the fewest migrants (23% of the population).

Although the traditional sector had the lowest actual number of migrants, they were, however, the most mobile, making 1.43 journeys each (Table 7). In the modern capitalist sector, with the highest percentage of families with migrants, the mobility was lowest, at 1.03 journeys each. This figure was also substantially lower than that for the smallholding sector. The higher migration of the population in the modern capitalist sector may have resulted from its dependence upon wage labour, and the need to seek a salary regardless of geographical distance.

In the three sectors, the destination of 45–49% of the migratory flow was other departments. In the modern capitalist sector, 69% of migrants went to urban areas. In the traditional capitalist sector, of the total movement to urban areas, 73% went to cities in other departments. In that sector, this pattern is repeated with rural migration, implying that much long-distance displacement occurs among family units that are remote from the central routes of the zone. Such displacements possibly result from the pull of other coffee-growing areas that need specialized labour. The opposite tendency can be observed in the modern capitalist sector where rural and urban destinations that attract family units are in the same department.

In the traditional capitalist sector, 66% of the moves were for periods of over 1 year. In the modern sector, the figure dropped to 59%, and in the smallholding sector, to 54%. On the other hand, movements lasting 1–3 months accounted for almost 20% in the modern sector, but only 14% in the traditional capitalist sector. In all three sectors, however, migration tended to be more permanent than temporary.

The greatest number of migrants came from families in which the household head was employed directly in farming. Of the total migrants, 79% of those in the modern, 76% in the traditional, and 67% in the small-

Table 7. Migration by place and area of destination and sector (% distribution).

	Smallholding sector	Traditional capitalist	Modern capitalist
Number of journeys per migrant	1.23	1.43	1.03
Migration to other departments	48.2	48.8	45.3
Migration to other municipalities in the same department	51.8	51.2	54.6
Migration to urban areas	41.7	46.1	69.2
In other departments	32.1	73.1	33.3
In the same department	67.9	26.9	66.6
Migration to rural areas	58.2	53.9	30.8
In other departments	42.3	64.0	36.1
In the same department	57.5	36.0	63.9
Total migratory movements	100	100	100

Table 8. *Distribution of families (%) by sector and number of children who have died.*

	Smallholding sector	Traditional capitalist	Modern capitalist
Families in which no children died	61.1	65.8	75.7
Families in which children died	38.9	34.2	24.3
Number of children who died			
1	49.4	50.0	60.0
2	26.6	26.2	25.7
3	13.9	14.3	8.6
4	2.5	7.1	5.7
above 4	7.6	2.4	0.0

holding sector came from such families. Migration in the smallholding and modern sectors tended to be typical of the lowest income segment of the population: 47% of the migrants from the smallholding sector and 53% from the modern sector came from families in which the income of the household head was below COP 10 000/month. In the traditional capitalist sector, on the other hand, more than 50% of migrants came from families with a monthly income above COP 20 000. The reasons for migration were primarily economic: 66% of migrants in the smallholding sector and 80% in the modern sought work and better pay whereas, in the traditional sector, that figure fell to 48%. Other motives, such as accompanying one's family (24%) or seeking education (13%), were also relevant.

Finally, some characteristics of morbidity and mortality were considered (Table 8). The percentage of families in which one or more children had died varied from 39% in the smallholding sector to 24% in the modern sector. Of those families that had lost children, 60% in the modern sector had lost only one child, whereas over 50% in the smallholding sector had lost more than one child. Multiple deaths had occurred in these families: 7% of smallholding families had lost more than five children.

CONCLUSION

This paper began with three main hypotheses concerning the relationship between economic and demographic behaviour in Colombia, which may now be examined in the light of the above findings. The search for a salary was maintained to be the major determinant of a family's economic and demographic behaviour and organization. More specifically, the hypotheses were:

- Families in the modern capitalist sector would tend to migrate within and between regions in response to the demand for labour, and their urban and modern orientation would result in lower fertility.
- Smallholding families would have a stable and relatively numerous family unit. Migration would be less prevalent, mainly by children who were a burden upon the family's resources, and would tend to be intraregional.

71

- The traditional capitalist sector would be characterized by seasonal migration, permanent migration would be less common, and fertility would be high relative to the modern sector.

An important and unexpected finding of this study was the relative affluence and stability of the traditional capitalist sector compared with the smallholding and modern capitalist sectors. The families depended upon the cultivation and sale of coffee as well as other crops; hence, a steady and reliable income was obtained and unemployment was rare. Family labour, both paid and unpaid, was used as required, and was particularly prevalent among middle producers where the hiring of salaried labour was relatively infrequent. In the smallholding sector, by contrast, the small area of landholdings and the uncertainty of rental arrangements on which many families depended led to considerable unemployment and insecurity. In the modern capitalist sector, the reliance on wage labour also created considerable unemployment and instability.

As hypothesized, fertility differed according to sector, with the smallholding sector having the largest number of children per family. However, contrary to expectation, the two capitalist sectors had almost identical fertility patterns. Within all three sectors, family size declined as income and area of landholding increased. When broken down by income and landholding categories, in most cases, the traditional capitalist sector had the smallest number of children. Among the largest landowners, for example, this sector had an average of 0.5 fewer children than their modern capitalist counterparts. The relative well-being and security of the traditional capitalist sector compared with the other two groups perhaps explains this unexpected finding.

Sectoral differences were also found with regard to employment opportunities and migration patterns. Contrary to expectations, the traditional capitalist, not the smallholding, sector had the lowest level of migration. Again, the relatively stable employment and income of this group seems to explain this outcome. Also, migration patterns of members of this sector were more permanent than in other groups, and often for reasons other than economic.

As expected, migration was more prevalent in the modern sector but, surprisingly, modern capitalist migrants tended to remain in the "home" department more than migrants from the other two sectors. Perhaps this was due to the low educational levels of migrants in the modern sector which would tend to limit their marketability in areas far removed from their native territory.

Thus, it may be concluded that the impact of modernization in the agricultural sector is not as unilineal as might be expected. In many families interviewed in this investigation, considerable disruption to family life and opportunities for income generation had been experienced as a result of modernization. It was, in fact, in the traditional capitalist farmers that had not yet modernized that the greatest security, in terms of economic and familial stability, was observed. The implications of this finding have not been examined here but should certainly be explored in future studies of the economic and demographic characteristics of Colombia's agricultural sector.

DEMOGRAPHIC STRATEGIES IN AN UNDERDEVELOPED REGION OF A MODERN COUNTRY: THE CASE OF SANTIAGO DEL ESTERO, ARGENTINA

Floreal H. Forni and Roberto Benencia

Families and households are the most fundamental decision-making units of the economy determining a vast array of economic behaviour, including labour supply, commodity demand, population growth, mobility, and savings. The family, by a complex set of processes, determines its size and composition, the allocation of each household member's time, its geographic location, and its expenditures. Few individuals ever make these decisions in vacuo during any part of their lives. Most of these decisions are jointly determined within the household and are, as well, interrelated over time. For example, the labour force participation of various household members is the result of interconnected decisions and is also dependent upon future choices (Goldin 1981).

Modern Argentina is the product of two principal demographic processes. The first was the Spanish colonization of the northern provinces with its accompanying cultural and economic changes; the second was the large influx of European immigrants, mainly of Mediterranean origin, into Buenos Aires and the Pampean region at the end of the 19th century. The development of the rich land of the Pampean region had important implications for the northern provinces of Tucumán and Santiago del Estero. The former specialized in sugar cultivation; the latter, in forest exploitation to provide wood for the railways that were being built to connect the northern and southern provinces.

Important migratory movements, both of a seasonal and permanent nature, have characterized Santiago del Estero from as early as the beginning of the 19th century. Tucumán's sugar crops employed a large proportion of the seasonal migrants, as did, somewhat later, cotton production in the neighbouring province of Chaco. The Pampean region also attracted migrants for cereal harvesting, especially after World War I. Finally, after World War II, migration to metropolitan Buenos Aires increased as demand for seasonal labour declined with the mechanization of agriculture in areas of previously high labour demand. Consequently, the rural population of Santiago del Estero decreased between 1947 and 1960 mainly as a result of emigration. By the time of the 1980 census, however, the rural population of the province seemed to have stabilized

73

Table 1. Total and rural populations ('000) of the departments of Rio Hondo and Robles, Santiago del Estero Province, and of the country, 1914–1980.

Year	Rio Hondo	Rural		Robles	Rural		Santiago del Estero	Rural		Country	Rural	
	Population	Number	%	Population	Number	%	Population	Number	%	Population	Number	%
1914	11.8	11.8	100	11.3	11.3	100	261.7	225.1	86	7903.7	3727.4	47
1947	26.8	22.1	82	19.6	16.4	84	479.5	358.1	75	15893.8	5961.7	38
1960	21.8	14.4	66	18.6	15.5	83	476.5	298.7	63	20013.8	5252.2	26
1970	27.7	16.3	59	22.3	15.1	68	495.4	272.0	55	23364.4	4386.0	19
1980	38.8	18.2	47	26.8	15.6	58	594.9	285.6	48	27947.4	4772.3	17

Source: Argentina (1914, 1947, 1960, 1970, 1980).

because of greater agricultural development in the region (Table 1). This included irrigation of a large area surrounding the Rio Dulce and emphasis on horticultural production involving the intensive use of labour.

SOCIOECONOMIC AND DEMOGRAPHIC CHARACTERISTICS OF SELECTED COMMUNITIES

The rural population of Santiago del Estero is characterized by high fertility and migration and, hence, acts as a permanent source of unskilled labour for the more-developed regions of the country. Public policies have actually encouraged high fertility through a system of salary increments based on a worker's family size. On the other hand, the population is in constant contact with other areas of the country where lower fertility is prevalent, and relatives of Santiago del Estero residents have distinctly smaller families. Hence, this province is an interesting area for research on demographic strategies in circumstances where social development is low but developmental influences of an economic nature are nonetheless considerable.

The sites selected for the study were two rural communities, each about 50 km from the capital city of Santiago del Estero, in the departments of Rio Hondo and Robles.

RIO HONDO

Rio Hondo is characterized by dry land with very little agricultural potential. The traditional activity is extensive cattle-raising, and small kitchen gardens are maintained for domestic consumption. In recent years, the cycle of rains has changed somewhat and capitalist agriculture has begun to permeate the region. The main crops produced have been export products including soya, sorghum, and beans. This production is concentrated in the hands of capitalist enterprises, usually outsiders to the area. Thus, the population consists mainly of poor rural families relying on seasonal migration, usually to work in Tucumán's sugar crops, for their subsistence.

Although unable to secure stable employment from their own agricultural land, Rio Hondo families could count on fairly secure incomes as a result of two main circumstances. During the 1940s, the first Peronist government instituted several reforms in favour of the workers. These included the establishment of collective conventions, unionization, payment of salaries in cash, and introduction of social services. This allowed seasonal migrants to earn sufficient incomes to survive during the slack season, and to supplement these with earnings from other sources during nonharvest periods. Moreover, the work in Tucumán's sugar plantations, although arduous, was not viewed as a hardship, but was eagerly awaited year after year because the whole family participated as a team, the wife usually responsible for the preparation of food. Daily life in the workers' camps was permeated by social harmony and entertainment.

The second factor affecting the well-being of Rio Hondo families was the introduction of food and hotel industries into the area. Rio Hondo became, during the 1950s, a winter tourist centre complementary to Mar del Plata in the summer. Toward the end of the 1960s, the sugar industry experienced a severe crisis, which continues today. The effort to increase productivity included greater mechanization of the harvest, resulting in a constant decline in the demand for labour. This led the search for jobs to diversify more toward the food and hotel sector, construction activities, and harvests in other provinces. Nonetheless, these families still tend to look to Tucumán sugar crops as their primary source of subsistence. This is explained partly by the social services provided for the whole family because of the father's participation (the father being the only registered worker), partly by the opportunity for the whole family to participate, and partly, perhaps, by proximity, habit, and lack of other occupational skills.

ROBLES

Located in the heart of Rio Dulce's irrigation area, Robles is heavily dependent upon agriculture and constitutes one of the major food-producing areas in the province (Table 2). The dominant social class is the small peasantry, some in partnership with landowners, others as labourers on

Table 2. Main agricultural products of Rio Hondo and Robles (in % of gross value of production [GVP] and GVP per hectare in "pesos") in 1914, 1937, and 1969.

Product	Rio Hondo	Robles	Province
1914			
Cows	38	46	
Sweet potato	25	33	
Wool	24	15	
Corn	6	0	
GVP per hectare	2.5	3.6	1.9
1937			
Cows	37	7	
Milk	22	0	
Sheep, mutton, wool	25	0	
Pig	7	0	
Alfalfa	0	27	
Cotton	0	19	
Garlic	0	9	
Wheat	0	8	
Potato	0	5	
GVP per hectare	14.5	18.0	4.7
1969			
Calabash	21	6	
Alfalfa	16	23	
Cows	14	0	
Milk	9	0	
Corn	7	5	
Tomato	0	22	
Sweet potato	0	13	
Onion	0	6	
Wheat	0	5	
Cotton	0	5	
GVP per hectare	7.8	56.9	3.7

Source: Forni and Benencia (1983).

the larger cotton estates. As the price of cotton declined, horticulture grew in importance, accompanied by heavy demands for capital and labour at peak periods during the year. This led to a precarious economic situation for increasing numbers of seasonal workers, dependent on wage work, but nonetheless retaining their small plots of land.

Mention should also be made of a settlement, Colonia El Simbolar, comprising 400 farms in parcels of 25 ha. This was instituted by the government to provide compensation to small farmers who had sold their holdings to make way for irrigation and large commercial estates. Considerable diversification in labour and land use resulted. Families with fewer resources often rented their land to others and worked for wages themselves; others employed numerous workers on their plots. In spite of such diversification, the peasantry remained tied to their land both in El Simbolar and in the irrigation area, some as nonfarming residents, others working as "part-time peasants."

METHODOLOGY

The research design consisted of three stages. First, a family register was constructed for the province as a whole, based upon the National Population Census of 1970. A typology of families based on size and composition was constructed from the census data. Second, a stratified sample of 545 households was selected within the communities of Rio Hondo and Robles (of families in four occupational categories: peasants [100 households], settlers [122 households], temporary workers in the irrigation area [200 households], and migrant workers in Tucumán [123 households]). Information was collected on fertility, migration, family size and structure, occupational patterns, and other economic and social characteristics. Finally, case studies were conducted with selected families of the same occupational categories. These case studies were conducted by participant observation and intensive interviews, the researchers residing with some of the families for several days.

Through these data, social, economic, and demographic data on the families and the interrelations of members' activities could be interpreted more meaningfully in terms of their overall survival strategies. This would not have been possible if the analysis had been based on secondary and survey data alone.

HOUSEHOLD SURVIVAL STRATEGIES

The daily behaviour of domestic groups is organized to balance production and consumption of resources through the division of household labour, both within and outside the home. These are referred to here as survival strategies, which also encompass a range of responsibilities

Table 3. Household composition and size in study areas, 1982, and in departments, province, and nationally, 1980 (% of total households).

Household composition[a]	Country	Province	Rio Hondo		All households	Robles		
			All households	Wage workers		Settlers	Peasants	Wage workers
Nuclear complete	58.1	41.8	42.3	62.0	43.6	78.0	49.0	54.0
Nuclear incomplete	8.2	11.9	13.4	7.0	10.2	5.0	9.0	13.0
Extended	22.3	30.5	31.5	10.0	30.5	12.0	20.0	15.0
Complex	11.5	15.8	12.7	20.0	15.7	6.0	21.0	18.0
Total	100.0	100.0	100.0	100.0	100.0	100.0	100.0	100.0
Number of households	–	–	–	123.0	–	122.0	100.0	200.0
Mean number of household members[b]	3.8	4.7	4.7	6.2	4.7	5.2	4.9	5.5

[a]Definitions: Nuclear complete = Father and mother with children; Nuclear incomplete = Only father or mother with children; Extended = Nuclear complete or incomplete with grandparents; and Complex = Nuclear (complete or incomplete) or extended with other relatives or nonrelatives.
[b]Not included in this classification are "one-person households."

among family members, both resident and nonresident. These arrangements are essentially normative or socially defined, and are modified periodically according to changes in surrounding circumstances, whether economic, social, political, or ecological.

These broad strategies and their relationship to demographic characteristics in the selected areas of Santiago del Estero are described here. These are analyzed according to the four principal occupational groups in these communities: wage workers of Rio Hondo (the dry area), settlers, small peasants, and wage workers of Robles (the irrigation area). The demographic factors examined include household composition, migration and division of family labour, and fertility.

HOUSEHOLD COMPOSITION

Families were predominantly nuclear in all occupational groups (Table 3). The settlers in the irrigated area, Robles, have the highest proportion of nuclear families (83%) but, in all cases, these are the majority. Because settlers are the most economically secure, the need for support, both of themselves and their children, is less than among peasants and wage workers where families apparently band together for security and economy. In many cases, extended families consisted of grandparents taking care of grandchildren or distantly related foster children while parents were absent for seasonal or permanent work outside the community. Thus, joint family arrangements prevailed among landless and land-poor families in which the labour of each member was an important part of the family's short- and long-term strategies for subsistence.

MIGRATION AND DIVISION OF FAMILY LABOUR

The survival strategies of wage workers in Rio Hondo were characterized by the combined labour of the whole family, including seasonal migration to Tucumán sugar plantations during the harvest period, and subsistence farming and handicraft production during the rest of the year. The participation of female household members in these activities was significant: women were registered as economically active in 90% of the households. The labour of children on family plots and the contributions of migrant family members were also considerable. These strategies not only maximized the use of family labour but preserved the cohesive character of family ties and traditions.

In the case of the Robles settlers, the term "survival strategies" is not applicable because these horticultural settlers earned incomes and enjoyed a standard of living substantially higher than those of the other occupational groups. Spouses participated in extradomestic activities in only about 25% of the families, and the work of children was negligible. Labour migration was also the least of all groups, mainly because of the value placed upon education by settler families. Hence, resident and outmigrating children were expected to devote their efforts to longer-term, educational investments.

Labour in the peasant households in Robles consisted mainly of the work of the family head, assisted occasionally (in about 25% of the cases)

Table 4. Mean number of live-born children by age group of mother in four occupational groups, 1982.

Mother's age group (years)	Rio Hondo				Robles						Total	
	Wage workers		Settlers		Peasants		Wage workers		All households			
	Children	Number of women	Children	Number of women	Children	Number of women	Children	Number of women	Children	Number of women	Children	Number of women
15–24	0.367	79	0.694	36	0.591	22	1.145	62	0.908	120	0.693	199
25–34	4.742	31	2.614	44	1.769	13	3.423	52	2.899	109	3.307	140
35–44	7.042	24	4.947	19	3.714	21	5.438	48	4.920	88	5.375	112
45–49	7.579	19	5.105	19	4.765	17	7.158	19	5.709	55	6.189	74

by the spouse and, only rarely, by small children. Migration, however, was an important strategy among older offspring, who apparently followed a pattern of "relay migration" (Arizpe 1975), in which one son or daughter migrated to relieve the labour surplus on the farm and to provide remittances from jobs obtained elsewhere. When this son or daughter married, or for some other reason could not continue to send funds home, another family member migrated outward, releasing his or her sibling from former obligations.

As with the peasants, families of Robles wage workers depended principally on the labour of the household head; spouses participated in the labour force in only about 10% of the families interviewed. Although children's work was somewhat more substantial than among the other Robles groups, it existed in only 18% of households. Dependence upon migrant contributions was also considerably less than among wage workers in Rio Hondo. Hence, the survival strategies of wage labourers in the irrigation area more closely resembled those of the families of small peasants than of wage labourers in the dry zone. This is perhaps because of the greater proximity and abundance of seasonal work in the richer irrigated area.

FERTILITY

Santiago del Estero is a province with high fertility in comparison to national levels, and there is evidence that fertility has even increased slightly during the last 15 years. Moreover, fertility in the two study areas was higher than that of the province as a whole. The fertility of the interviewed population was estimated at 5.4 live-born children per woman as opposed to 4.9 for the province, and 2.9 for the nation, in 1981.

Fertility differed considerably between wage workers in both areas and the other two groups, an average gap of over two children (Table 4). Peasants have the lowest fertility of all categories. Therefore, settler and peasant couples were apparently using some form of fertility control, whereas wage workers did not appear to be doing so.

Although contraceptive use was not investigated in this study, birth spacing indicated that it was greatest among settlers and peasants. Probably, then, some artificial control of fertility was used by these groups. Also, the wage workers in the nonirrigated area, Rio Hondo, appeared to delay childbearing, although their completed fertility was the highest of all groups. This may mean that birth control may have been practiced in the early years of marriage by couples in this class.

A possible explanation for these differences in fertility is that, for peasants and settlers, a large number of children would complicate the process of inheritance and subdivision of land among offspring. For the wage-working families, on the other hand, a larger number of children would result in higher total household incomes.

An interesting finding of the analysis of births among the population in the irrigated area was the preponderance of sons in all three groups. A tentative explanation is that the size of the family was influenced by

81

the number of sons among the first births: the higher the proportion of males in the first three births, the larger the total family size. Thus, couples who had borne several sons early in the childbearing period apparently had more children than those who had an early history of female births. Other researchers have explained similar observations of an unbalanced sex ratio in the region by possible neglect of daughters or infanticide, but no evidence of these practices was found in the present study. In fact, equal affection seemed to be accorded to children of both sexes among all the groups studied.

CONCLUSION

What conclusions can be drawn concerning the influence of rural development on demographic behaviour in the sampled areas of Santiago del Estero?

First, social class or economic status seemed to be a more important determinant of family size and demographic choices than the level of social and economic development in the two areas. In other words, wage earners in both irrigated and nonirrigated areas had similar fertility and migration patterns, whereas these differed markedly from peasants in the higher occupational or landowning categories.

Second, demographic strategies seemed to be rationally interrelated and also related to economic circumstances. For example, household composition could be interpreted as an adaptive response to the opportunities and uncertainties of prevailing economic circumstances. Nuclear families predominated among all groups, but the tendency was greatest among the settlers in the irrigated areas, whose children migrated to pursue education rather than agricultural activities. This reflected the greater security of these peasant households and the possibility of long-range planning for their offspring. Wage earners, on the other hand, required more immediate support from a large number of children to ensure adequate subsistence incomes for the family. These children were often somewhat removed from the immediate nuclear group. Fertility and migration could thus also be said to be interrelated in a broadly rational manner.

Although it is tempting to emphasize these inherent complementarities and their rationality, the behaviour of the surveyed population cannot be viewed merely as a calculation of optimization of benefits. The dynamic interrelationships between fertility and migration, as well as the interaction of demographic and economic factors, must also be seen in the context of cultural practices and other social and environmental conditions, many of which have been neglected here. Frequently, such behaviour is a response to unforeseen or uncontrollable events, or combinations thereof, which demographic generalizations or models of behaviour should never be so rigid as to ignore.

FAMILY AND LABOUR IN RURAL PERU: NEW INTERPRETATIONS

Carlos E. Aramburú

This chapter examines how rural Peruvian families cope with changing agrarian policies and capitalist expansion in their daily lives. The discussion focuses on rural households in four regions and their adaptation to the external and internal constraints imposed by these changes.

The data for this analysis were gathered through a series of field studies starting in 1977 in the coastal valleys of Cañete and Bajo Piura and ending in 1979 in two zones in Puno, in the southern highlands of Peru (Aramburú and Ponce 1983). In 1980, an interdisciplinary team (directed by the author and coresearcher Ana Ponce) undertook the comparative analysis of this data. This report examines some of the findings and discusses two contrasting models of rural development and household strategies that characterize major trends of rural change in Peru and, to some extent, in Latin America.

METHODOLOGY

Two major problems became clear from the beginning of the study: how to account for social change, and what levels of analysis should be considered to describe such transformations. The four selected regions represented different levels of development and maximum variability in ecology, natural resource endowment, land tenure structure, crop patterns, and culture. Because rural Peru is extremely varied in almost every respect, however, the regions chosen cannot represent the whole of rural Peru. Within each region, the sample was designed to allow the greatest homogeneity of social class. Only rural households of independent small farmers directly involved in agriculture or animal husbandry were chosen (thus, households of rural labourers, cooperative members, and other types were excluded).

The aim was to study the effects of external (regional) and internal (familial) factors on household demographic, economic, and social strategies. A step-by-step analysis was conducted, starting with a historical overview of regional changes in land-use patterns, land-tenure systems, rural labour markets, and demographic dynamics in this century. Information was taken from previous regional studies and official sources such as agricultural and population censuses and agricultural statistics.

A comparison between rural households at increasingly disaggregated levels was then attempted. First, the basic demographic, economic, and social characteristics of households in each region were compared. Second, the rural households of each region were divided into three strata on the basis of five variables (educational level of household head, size of parcel, monetary family income, quality of housing, and household assets), and demographic, economic, and social behaviour were compared among strata of the same region. Finally, each stratum was compared across regions according to the same broad characteristics. The first and third steps allowed differences to be observed in household strategies, attributable to external (regional) factors, that controlled the internal (household) factors. The second step examined specifically how demographic, economic, and social strategies vary within a specific region among households with different internal characteristics.

The information for this comparative analysis of households between and within regions was taken from household surveys and in-depth interviews conducted with a sample of small-scale farmers in each of the four areas. The total sample consisted of 569 rural households.

REGIONAL TRANSFORMATIONS AND THE SMALL-SCALE FARMERS

In the abundant literature dealing with capitalist expansion in traditional rural societies, at least three types of processes have been noted (C. Scott 1976). The classical Marxist approach argues that concentrating land and expanding the capitalist market economy will eventually "decapitalize" the peasant economy through eviction, heavy debts, low productivity, and so on, finally leading to the "proletarianization" of the peasantry (Marx 1969).

A different perspective is offered by the concept of "marginality" developed mainly by the dependency school in Latin America (Matos Mar et al. 1969; Nun 1969), and some cultural anthropologists (Foster 1965; Holmberg et al. 1966; Mayer 1976). They argue that modernization does not necessarily mean traditional cultures are integrated into the mainstream of Western life and that, instead, pauperization without significant proletarianization is the rule in most Andean countries. The peasantry is left to survive with a shrinking resource base, and its existence is, to a large degree, marginal to the modernization process and to capital accumulation.

Yet a third perspective, developed recently by Latin American scholars, argues that capitalist development leads to structural heterogeneity and that certain modes of production (mainly the Andean peasantry) are formally subordinated to the capitalist economy, but maintain control over their land and their traditional relations of production (Bartra 1975; Bengoa 1979; Aramburú 1982).

This study showed that patterns of regional development vary significantly, and that no single model can account for this variability. In Cañete, the process of capitalist expansion has led to a transformation of tenants into farmers, who compete increasingly with the remaining haciendas. This agrees with the "farmers' road of capitalist development," proposed by Kautsky (1970) in his massive work, *La Cuestión Agraria*, referring to Germany and Europe. The regional economy is market oriented and market dominated, and modern institutions pervade.

In the Bajo Piura valley, the large estate still dominates the rural economy, and small farmers, as well as the landless rural population, are involved in the production of foodcrops for home consumption and of some cash crops (cotton) for the market. The main link with the estates is the seasonal labour market, where small farmers and their relatives seek employment during the cotton harvest and are paid on a piece-work basis. Thus, a complementary, albeit conflictive, relationship exists between the hacienda and the small farm. Many of the younger, better-educated workers have left the valley to seek their fortunes in the nearby city of Piura or in Lima, 1000 km south. Nevertheless, the rural majority still depends on the small family farm for subsistence: the regional labour market can provide wage employment for only part of the rural labour force part of the time. A process of semiproletarianization has thus emerged in this area over the past 60 years.

In the highlands of Puno, the Altiplano, the remaining peasant communities are marginal to the large ranching estates. Few employment opportunities exist in these firms for the Quechua and Aymara peasants; most of whom still cling to their minute family plots that are devoted almost entirely to the cultivation of Andean staples for household consumption using their traditional technology (such as the foot-plow). Most of these households are involved in seasonal long-distance migration either to urban centres on the coast and in the sierra, or to the nearby tropical colonization zones, where they engage in wage labour during the idle season in the Altiplano (from June through September). This case could best be described as pauperization without modernization, revealing yet another pattern of regional capitalist development in Peru.

Finally, in the tropical colonization zone of Puno (the Tambopata valley), the major modernization factor has been the expansion of coffee cultivation as the main cash crop. Small and medium farms are market oriented but still operate under traditional methods of production. Extended families are more common than in the highlands, and labour is still provided by the members of the household. No significant land or capital concentration has been observed, although internal differentiation among the farmers is significant and second only to the level found in Cañete. Tropical Puno thus exemplifies a fourth type of regional development pattern typical of frontier areas in the Peruvian Amazon.

Within these contrasting development contexts, rural households develop their survival strategies — how they cope with the external and internal constraints of their daily lives.

Rural Household Strategies: Two Tentative Models

The concept of survival strategies was generated in the context of specific behavioural patterns of poor urban households (Duque and Pastrana 1973). Since then it has been widely, and sometimes uncritically, adopted by social researchers in Latin America to describe very different types of behaviour, including decisions on fertility, migration, and occupational and social mobility (Martine 1979; Torrado 1981; Berquo and Loyola 1982).

This approach is popular because it attempts to overcome mechanistic and linear explanations of social behaviour, so common in the Marxist literature of the region. The main contention of the survival strategy approach is that individuals or families, despite their deprivation and poverty, are able to cope with the impact of capitalist development by creating alternative means of dealing with processes that may be disadvantageous to them in economic as well as sociocultural terms. A common example is the expansion of the informal and sometimes illegal economy in the urban sector, including petty trade, smuggling, and personal services. Growth of the informal economy is seen as a response to high unemployment rates, massive rural-to-urban migration, and the high concentration of income that prevails in these societies. Another example is circular and seasonal rural migration of poor peasants that enables them to take advantage of different harvest cycles and wage differentials, thus obtaining additional income that allows them to hold on to their small land parcels (Forni et al. 1984).

This perspective emphasizes the household as the relevant unit of analysis to understand survival strategies from both a methodological and cultural point of view. Methodologically, the household is treated as an intermediate level of analysis between the individual and the social class. Culturally, these studies emphasize the importance of kinship and affiliation to understanding economic and social behaviour among the poor classes of Latin America. This interest in family and kinship is certainly not new: anthropological studies have long advocated the study of kinship as a major issue in developing countries and traditional societies. What is new is that households are treated not individually but as belonging to a specific type or class, thus permitting a measure of collective behaviour.

Nevertheless, a major methodological problem is how to deal empirically with the household. Usually the data referring to characteristics of the household head are attributed to the family as a whole. Thus, the analysis operates at an individual and not an aggregate level. Matching the characteristics of the household head to the rest of the family members is an analytical alternative, but this is not a simple procedure. Furthermore, because different members of the household can have different "class situations," both economically and culturally, allotting specific households to a certain social class can be misleading and arbitrary. This remains a major challenge in this type of perspective (Mora y Araujo 1982).

Studies dealing with household strategies still reflect the different "styles" of either qualitative in-depth studies of a few cases, or large quantitative analyses of sample surveys of certain types of households. Our study falls largely within the second style of research. We have attempted to discover objective behaviour patterns emerging from sample data with respect to specific areas of conduct, such as fertility, migration, household composition, and working patterns. We assume a certain rationality and attribute it to specific households which, of course, does not consider the degree to which the social actors are deliberate about their behaviour and its consequences. Thus, the issue of choice among alternative behaviours is left aside. Even if sufficient data on the rationale behind alternative choices were available, the matching of this evidence to observed behaviour patterns would still be problematic because of the unconscious nature of many of these strategies. This aspect of survival strategy research is undoubtedly one of its major conceptual and methodological weaknesses.

BASIC CHARACTERISTICS OF REGIONS AND HOUSEHOLDS

Cañete has the best ecological conditions for irrigated agriculture of the four regions: over 77% of its soils are class 1 (Table 1); it has a stable climate (average yearly temperature, 19.7°C) and is located at sea level. The poorest zone, in terms of its ecological limitations for agriculture, is the Altiplano of Puno where only 3% of the soil is good for intensive agriculture, mean altitude is 4000 m, and temperature is low the year round with wide daily and seasonal variations (from −5°C to 22°C in the same day during the dry season, June–September). In Bajo Piura, the main limitations for agriculture are lack of water for irrigation and poor drainage. In tropical Puno, soil fertility is initially high but deteriorates rapidly under intensive cultivation, as most tropical acidic soils do.

The structure of land tenure varies significantly across the four regions. Land is least concentrated in Cañete where 89% of all farms have less than 5 ha but own about 24% of all arable land, and most concentrated in Bajo Piura and the Altiplano where farms under 5 ha account for 87 and 73% of all farms, respectively, but own only 7% of the land in each area.

Fertility patterns seem to be remarkably similar in the four regions (Table 2) and linked not to levels of development but to cultural factors. Thus, the Quechuas and Aymaras of the Altiplano and lowlands of Puno share a longer birth interval, slightly later age at marriage, and lower average number of surviving children. The coastal Mestizo population has a shorter birth interval and higher fertility.

Migration is high in both regions of Puno, although for different reasons. Outmigration from the Altiplano responds mainly to economic push factors whereas, in the colonization zone, it is related to pull factors associated with educational opportunities outside the region. Seasonal migration, on the other hand, seems linked to the level of regional development. One of every four household heads is involved in short-term seasonal migration in the poorest regions, Bajo Piura and the Altiplano of Puno. We shall see that seasonal movements are a basic household subsistence strategy for peasants in less-developed areas.

Table 1. Regional characteristics.

	More developed regions		Depressed regions	
Characteristics	Cañete	Tropical Puno[a]	Bajo Piura	Altiplano Puno
Ecology				
Altitude (m)	0	1750	0	4000
Mean annual temperature (°C)	19.7	28	23.7	5.5
Mean annual rainfall (mm)	27.9	2100	–	800
Soil types[b] (% of area)				
Class 1–3	77.2	8.2	45.0	3.1
Class 4	12.6	7.3	32.0	4.2
Class 5–6	10.2	84.5	23.0	91.8
Land tenure				
Farms under 1 ha				
% of total farms	53.8	25.2	60.4	29.6
% of total land	4.0	0.2	2.0	0.6
Farms 1–5 ha				
% of total farms	35.4	36.7	26.9	43.2
% of total land	19.6	2.6	5.3	6.1
Farms 5–500 ha				
% of total farms	10.7	37.2	12.6	26.5
% of total land	66.5	32.6	33.9	24.8
Farms above 500 ha				
% of total farms	0.1	0.8	0.2	0.6
% of total land	9.9	64.6	58.8	68.4
Population				
Total (1981)	57031	36605	100306	358881
% rural	48	89	60	81
Rural growth rate 1972–1981	1.8	5.1	-2.4	0.4
Sex ratio	106	119	98	93
% under 15 years	44	56	46	43
Crude birth rate[c]	31.0	35.5	33.0	34.2
Crude death rate[c]	5.0	16.1	13.0	11.2
Emigration rate (%)	11.8	13.9	23.3	23.1

Sources: Peru (1972a, b, 1981).
[a] Includes highland zones of the provinces of Sandia and Carabaya.
[b] Soil types are classified according to potential use. Classes 1–3 are considered good for intensive agriculture; class 4 is suitable for less intensive agriculture; and classes 5–6 are usable as pastureland or protection.
[c] Per thousand population.

Family structure is another dimension that seems related both to cultural factors (such as neolocal residence) and economic factors (such as lower monetary cost of housing in both areas of Puno). Thus, in the two coastal valleys (Cañete and Bajo Piura), extended families are found in more than half of the households, but nuclear families predominate among the Quechua and Aymara of Puno possibly because of neolocal residence patterns of new couples and the lower monetary cost of housing in these regions.

Literacy rates are higher in Cañete than in the other areas, and somewhat higher in the Altiplano of Puno than in Bajo Piura and tropical Puno. With the exception of Cañete, this suggests that educational attainment is only weakly related to regional development. The rural population of the Altiplano, although poor, has had access for a long time to formal

Table 2. Summary of sociodemographic and economic characteristics of households by region.

Characteristics	Regions by level of development			
	Cañete	Tropical Puno	Bajo Piura	Altiplano Puno
Fertility				
Average age of women in unions (years)	34.1	33.3	34.0	36.1
Median age at marriage (years)	21.1	21.3	20.6	21.4
Duration of union (years)	15.1	11.0	13.9	15.4
Average birth interval (years)	2.7	3.1	2.6	3.0
Average number of surviving children	4.1	3.7	4.5	3.6
Migration				
Permanent and temporary migrants (%)	4.3	12.2	7.8	19.0
Seasonal migrants (%)	–	14.0	25.0	26.0
Social				
Number of persons/house	6.3	6.7	7.2	6.0
% of extended families	51.3	30.0	58.2	20.8
% illiterate in population (over 6 years old)	5.1	24.0	25.3	19.4
Differentiation (ratio of high strata income/low strata income)	8.9	12.1	4.9	7.1
Economic				
Number of persons working/household	3.1	2.4	2.8	2.0
Activity rate (% of household members)	49.1	36.0	39.0	33.3
Household heads (%)				
With agriculture as main occupation	94.8	94.4	87.4	55.8
With secondary occupation	25.3	23.0	26.2	33.0
Using family workers	89.6	80.0	91.3	55.7
Hiring wage labour	75.7	51.0	57.3	19.9
Hiring permanent workers	33.3	4.1	12.7	12.2
Area under cultivation (ha)	4.5	2.0	2.6	1.7

education (in fact, highland Puno has two universities); in the colonization area, households enjoy better living standards but access to formal education is limited. Because economic opportunities in the Altiplano are no longer available, education is an asset in terms of outmigration to urban centres. Economic success in tropical Puno, by contrast, is related to agricultural experience and hard work, for which formal education is irrelevant.

Social relations of production centre around the family. The vast majority of households use unpaid family labour for productive activities. It is surprising that the lowest proportion is found in the Altiplano, where the traditional Quechua and Aymara cultures emphasize labour exchange and reciprocity. The main reason behind this unexpected finding is the absence of children and dependants of working age because of high emigration rates. This, as noted before, also affects the size of the household, its structure, and the number of workers per family. In fact, the Altiplano has the lowest average number of working persons per household (2.0, with an activity rate of 33%). The largest work force was found among the households of Cañete, with 3.1 economically active persons per household, and an activity rate of 49% of household members. Overall, a closer relationship seems to exist between the level of regional development and activity rates within the rural households compared to the weak relationship between fertility and regional development.

Although our sample was designed to include independent rural households only, not all the heads of families have agriculture as their main occupation. This is especially true in the Altiplano, where 44% of household heads have other main occupations such as livestock rearing, crafts, weaving, and fishing. Diversification is a central economic strategy in areas where agriculture is unreliable and of low economic potential, and survival frequently depends on having more than one occupation.

Finally, wage labour is also an important economic characteristic of rural households. Almost 76% of households in Cañete hire paid labourers, whereas only 20% do so in the Altiplano. Most of these workers are hired on a temporary basis only (Table 2). Regional differences are due not only to the availability of capital on the farm, but also to crop requirements. For example, coffee in Tambopata requires a large labour input only during harvest time, so the farms in this valley, despite their higher levels of capitalization, rarely hire permanent workers.

HOUSEHOLD STRATEGIES

The household strategies of the less-developed regions of Bajo Piura and the Altiplano are summarized in Appendix 1, and of the more-developed areas of Cañete and Tambopata, in Appendix 2. Because internal factors at the household level differ even within these areas, specific strategies also vary. The suggested models, however, are simplifications of actual observed patterns and, therefore, are still quite tentative in their content and implications.

The families of Bajo Piura and the Altiplano had the lowest living standards of all four regions. These regions also had the worst conditions for agriculture due to ecological limitations, a stagnant agricultural frontier, extreme land concentration, and few employment opportunities in agriculture. These were the main external constraints faced by the rural households. The characteristics of these families have already been described, including high emigration rates, small land holdings, dual-purpose agriculture (sale and consumption), low levels of technological innovation and capital accumulation, and little social differentiation.

The families of Cañete and Tambopata enjoy a much higher living standard than those of either Bajo Piura or the Altiplano, although for different reasons. In addition to the external factors that favour agricultural development in Cañete, it is characterized by better land distribution, proximity to the Lima market, and the prevalence of labour-intensive technological innovations. In the tropical colonization zone of Tambopata, the availability of rainfall, good initial soil fertility, an expanding agricultural frontier through spontaneous colonization, the predominance of medium and small property, and specialization in a high-value cash crop, such as coffee, are the major factors behind agricultural growth.

DEMOGRAPHIC STRATEGIES

Demographic strategies seem related more to migration and mobility than to fertility regulation. Average fertility was highest among the households of Bajo Piura, which had the lowest age at marriage and shortest birth intervals of all areas. Thus, the couples of this valley, the poorest in the sample, have the largest number of dependants and do not regulate their fertility. By contrast, the households of the Altiplano have the lowest fertility due to late marriage and a long birth interval. Late marriage seems to be related more to the inheritance pattern of the Altiplano, where a new couple can be established only after receiving land and other assets (cattle) from its parents, than to an explicit attempt to reduce fertility. Nevertheless, an average birth interval of 3.0 years suggests a high level of birth control. Other sources show that this region has one of the highest abortion rates in the country (Peru 1980).

As with the households in the poorer zones, no evidence of fertility regulation was observed in Cañete and Tambopata. The average number of surviving children to women in reproductive unions was 4.1 children in Cañete and 3.7 in Tambopata. Thus, these two regions have intermediate fertility levels, lower than Bajo Piura and slightly higher than the Altiplano.

Fertility was negatively correlated with socioeconomic status in all four regions (Table 3), the differentials being highest both in the more depressed area (the Altiplano) and in the more developed valley (Cañete). Perhaps the key factor behind this pattern is the educational level of the population. Even if unrelated to the level of regional development, education could explain fertility differentials because the women of both the Altiplano and Cañete were better educated than those in the other regions, and thus tended to marry later.

Compared to fertility regulation, migration was clearly an explicit strategy among the households of the depressed areas. The analysis distinguished between migration and mobility: the first referring to permanent or prolonged movements and the second to yearly seasonal migration to specific areas. Migration took the form of permanent expulsion of dependants in most of the rural households of the Altiplano and Bajo Piura; in fact, over 23% of natives in both valleys lived elsewhere at the time of the survey. In the Altiplano, over 81% of the households had at least one migrant over 15 years of age. The basic motivation was economic: seeking a new job or land (in the case of those moving to colonization zones from Altiplano Puno). The main destinations were Lima, for migrants from Bajo Piura, and Arequipa, Lima, and Tambopata, for those emigrating from the Altiplano.

Seasonal migration was clearly a common strategy in the Altiplano, but relatively rare in Bajo Piura. The peasants of the Altiplano migrated seasonally either to nearby colonization zones (such as the Tambopata valley) or to coastal rice plantations (in the valleys of Camana and Omate) during the slack season in the Altiplano (Martinez 1969; Collins 1983). In these areas, most worked as seasonal labourers and were paid on a piecework basis. This was the main source of cash for these migrants. Seasonal

91

Table 3. Household characteristics by zones and strata.[a]

Variables/strata	Bajo Piura			Altiplano Puno			Cañete			Tropical Puno		
	High	Middle	Low	High	Middle	Low	High	Middle	Low	High	Middle	Low
Average number of surviving children	3.6	4.3	4.8	3.1	3.4	4.4	3.2	4.0	4.4	3.4	3.5	4.2
Size of farms (ha)	3.8	1.9	0.5	7.8	3.0	0.9	9.7	3.6	1.2	7.5	2.6	0.8
% of farms having cash crops	58	38	12	27	23	8	100	97	90	97	89	79
% of household heads												
With more than one job	21	35	42	50	42	56	18	28	40	15	27	38
Hiring seasonal workers	92	46	23	32	15	12	94	74	47	63	52	63
Ratio of low/higher monetary income households	4.7	2.4	1.0	7.0	3.2	1.0	8.9	2.7	1.0	12.1	3.3	1.0

a The strata were constructed by area under cultivation.

migrants were older males, usually household heads, having low educational levels but belonging to the middle and, to a lesser extent, upper strata within the region. As discussed elsewhere (Aramburú 1982), permanent and seasonal migrations are combined strategies used to balance a household's supply of and demand for labour. The equilibrium point is determined by the annual average of endogenous labour demand: excess supply will result in permanent emigration of dependants, whereas seasonal deficits or surpluses will be handled by hiring temporary wage labourers or seasonal outmigration, respectively.

In Bajo Piura, seasonal migration during the cotton harvest was a move from small family plots to large cooperative estates within the valley for short periods (rarely more than 1 month). In contrast to the seasonal migrants of the Altiplano, mainly younger dependants of the poorer strata were involved in these short-distance labour movements. This was also a strategy to increase the household's source of cash and maximize the use of its labour force.

Migration, either permanent or seasonal, was of little importance among the households of the developing regions. Total emigration rates were 11.8% in Cañete and 13.9% in Tambopata, less than 50% of those recorded in the depressed areas. Around 4% of household members were temporarily absent in both regions, mainly for educational purposes. Nevertheless, most household heads in the colonization zones had migrated into this area from the Altiplano and had permanent residence there at the time of the survey. By contrast, most of the farmers in Cañete were native to the valley. Inmigration, as noted before, had been important in Cañete during the 1960s and early 1970s as a result of the collectivization of the haciendas by the military Agrarian Reform. Most of these recent migrants became workers of the new rural cooperatives and did not own land in the valley. In Tambopata, seasonal migration still occurs, but consists mainly of Andean peasants who descend into the valley to harvest coffee and then return to the Altiplano (Martinez 1969). In sum, demographic strategies in the more-developed zones were not as important in contrast to the more-depressed areas: neither fertility regulation nor migration were critical for household survival.

ECONOMIC STRATEGIES

Economic strategies were based on diversification of crops and economic activities among the households of the poorer regions. This was related to the small land area owned by the family: in Bajo Piura, 63% of the households had less than 2 ha with average plots of only 0.88 ha. These households owned only 21% of available agricultural land in the valley. The scarcity of land was also dramatic in the Altiplano: 48% of the peasant families had less than 2 ha, with average plots of only 0.87 ha. They owned only 21% of usable land in this region, which also had very low productivity per hectare due to climatic constraints and absence of irrigation.

Amount of land and capital determines the double role of peasant agriculture consumption and sale. Because consumption is based on cultural demands for various agricultural and dairy products, diversification of crops and herds serves both purposes. In the Altiplano, 67% of the households had three or more main crops on their land, mostly for their own consumption (such as quinoa, barley, and native tubers). Potatoes are the main cash crop, but only 22% of potato crop is sold in the market. In fact, some families are so poor that they must buy the same crops they cultivate to meet their consumption needs during part of the year. In Bajo Piura, 53% of the households had three or more main crops on their land. Cotton, all of which is sold in the local market, is the main cash crop and is cultivated exclusively for sale by over 93% of the farms. Food crops (such as beans and corn) were cultivated exclusively for consumption by three out of four households.

Economic innovation and specialization were perhaps the most important strategies among households in Cañete and Tambopata. These included specialization in commercial agriculture and adoption of modern inputs to increase land productivity. The first factor that permits this is the availability of agricultural land with productive potential: 46% of farms in Cañete have 2–6 ha, representing about 35% of the agricultural land in the valley. In Tambopata, family plots are small: 50% of the farms have less than 3 ha but have generally good conditions for coffee, the main cash crop. Marketing is a serious problem because of bad roads, long distances to market, and a monopsonic market, tied to loans from the state-owned Banco Agrario (Collins 1983).

Crop specialization is devoted to food crops in Cañete, especially high-value food and industrial crops under an agricultural system based on successive rotations of associated crops on the same field. Thus, at any time of year, each plot has at least two crops (for example, maize and beans, or apples and pears). They are replaced by two or more short-term crops during the rest of the agricultural year (if such crops are seasonal). This intensive method of cultivation, in terms of both land and labour, is found in 45% of small farms. Almost all the harvest is sold to local intermediaries or industrial processing plants. This type of agriculture relies heavily on industrial inputs and partial mechanization (for field preparation).

In tropical Puno, over 76% of the farmers had over 57% of their land planted with coffee, revealing the predominance of a specialized monocrop agricultural system. All the harvest was sold to a state cooperative or, in smaller proportions, to independent wholesalers. Most producers had to sell to the state cooperative because credit was tied to marketing arrangements through this agency. Despite the commercial nature of regional agriculture, the technology used was basic; only about 3% of farmers used any type of mechanization for land clearing, and almost 70% did not use any type of fertilizer or pesticide. Harvest was done entirely by hand and yields depended heavily on type of soil and climatic conditions. Without improved marketing, credit mechanisms, and guaranteed prices, the incentives for on-farm investment were low and accumulation was devoted primarily to financing nonagricultural, mainly commercial, activities.

Economic diversification also involved the performance of different jobs by household members in the poorer zones. One out of three family heads in the Altiplano, and one out of four in Bajo Piura, had two or more different jobs. In the Altiplano, secondary occupations were also based on the

94

domestic economy, such as cattle raising, weaving, pottery, fishing, and seasonal wage labour. In Bajo Piura, secondary jobs were related to trading and to the availability of temporary jobs in nearby towns and villages (in construction, carpentry, fish factories, and so on). Multiple jobs were clearly associated with low economic status in Bajo Piura: over 42% of household heads of the lower strata had more than one occupation, whereas only 21% of those of the upper strata had a secondary job (Table 3). In the Altiplano, however, 50% of household heads belonging to the upper strata had more than one occupation, compared to 56% in the lower and 42% in the middle strata. This was related to the employment opportunities in each region: in the Altiplano, nonagricultural employment is scarce; hence, wealthier families diversified into livestock, trade, and commercial activities. Poor families emigrated seasonally or took up traditional crafts. In Bajo Piura, the relatively rich specialized in cash agriculture, whereas the very poor lacked capital or land to specialize in cotton production and had to stay with food crops or emigrate seasonally or permanently. It was the middle peasant in the Altiplano who diversified the least, taking up traditional occupations such as weaving and pottery.

As a result of this emphasis on cash agriculture, occupational specialization was the predominant strategy among the households of the more-developed areas. About 95% of household heads in both Cañete and Tambopata worked permanently on the family farm. Only one household head of four in Cañete, and one of five in Tambopata had secondary occupations. This pattern was clearly associated with economic status in both regions, because poorer households had to diversify toward nonagricultural employment to augment low agricultural incomes.

The occupations of household members other than the household head were also analyzed, including those of the spouse and older children. Over 56% of spouses in Bajo Piura and 85% in the Altiplano performed economic activities related to agriculture and other domestic tasks. In the valley, 55% of household members worked as unpaid family labour in agriculture. In the Altiplano, only 25% of dependants worked as unpaid family labour, over 54% having independent jobs as herders or craftworkers, or owning their own plot of land. This suggests that on-farm employment prevails among upper strata families in more-developed regions (as we shall confirm later with Cañete and Tambopata), where economic diversification by household heads depends, among other things, on help from family members. Among the more deprived families in the poorest regions, economic diversification and independent activities characterized all family members who were economically active.

Social relations of production were centred around the family as in the least-developed zones: over 89% of household heads in Cañete and 80% in Tambopata used unpaid family labour in their productive activities. Around 95% of these workers were members of the nuclear family. In Tambopata, about 12% of unpaid family workers, such as sons-in-law, nieces, cousins, and brothers, belonged to extended families. Thus, kinship considerations are a constant feature of rural life in Peru and a strategy to diminish monetary costs of labour on the family farm.

The major difference from the stagnant rural zones was the greater use of wage labour, at least in Cañete. Of the small farmers of this valley, almost 68% hired additional workers, two-thirds of them temporarily. Furthermore, 33% of farmers had stable wage workers (two on average), whereas this characteristic is almost absent in every other region studied. This demonstrates the higher level of capital accumulation of Cañete farmers and their more "capitalistic" nature. Use of permanent wage labourers was associated with the amount of land cultivated; only 10% of farms with less than 2 ha had permanent workers, whereas 71% of those with over 6 ha had them. Wage labour, therefore, functions as a substitute for family labour when the area owned is too great to be cultivated by family workers alone, or when dependants are away pursuing education or better jobs. This also suggests the existence in Cañete of a rural labour market that, although still seasonal, is becoming increasingly stabilized due to the capitalization of small farming and multicropping. Cañete seems to typify the "farmers' road to development" and rural change in the central coastal valleys of Peru.

In Tambopata, wage labourers were employed on 51% of farms, over 93% of which hired only during harvest time. Permanent workers were almost nonexistent because coffee requires little care between harvests, and pruning and weeding were performed by family members. Thus, wage labour in this valley operates as a complement to and not a substitute for family workers. As in Cañete, larger farms (over 6 ha) hired permanent workers, but in a much smaller proportion; less than one in four families had them in Tambopata. Hence, in Tambopata, the domestic economy still dominates in spite of the predominance of cash agriculture and significant levels of capital accumulation.

Economic diversification is, therefore, a common strategy in depressed areas, but it varies by strata and among regions. In Bajo Piura, it is based on food crop diversification and temporary nonskilled farm jobs. In the Altiplano, it relies on seasonal migration to unskilled rural labour markets, other household activities, and expulsion of dependants either to the cities or to self-generated employment for the poorest families. Social relations of production also involve different family strategies. The main asset (or liability) of the household is its own labour force. As has been discussed frequently in the literature, labour costs to the peasant economy are fixed in the short run and are equivalent to average consumption, not to the current wage, and so are independent of its productivity (Millar 1970; Bengoa 1979; Aramburú 1982). This means that the household can minimize labour costs by maximizing the use of unpaid family labour, especially if the opportunity cost for labour is low.

Our survey showed that unpaid family labour is widely used by rural households: around 90% of households relied on family workers as their main source of labour, regardless of the level of regional development. The sole exception was in the Altiplano of Puno, where about 44% of the households did not use family labour (Table 2). The reason seems to be that most of the dependants of working age had emigrated or had independent occupations. Also, the small size of the parcel and low productivity require less labour inputs per unit area than anywhere else. Unpaid labourers are recruited predominantly from among the members of the nuclear family: 97% of these were either the spouse or children in Bajo Piura, and 89% of the unpaid workers belonged to the nuclear family in the Altiplano, where an additional 11% were relatives not belonging to the households.

The use of wage labourers is common in Bajo Piura, on over 53% of the farms whereas, in the Altiplano, only 20% of farms had any paid workers. Most of this wage labour is seasonal: over 87% of the farms hiring workers in Bajo Piura, and 80% in the Altiplano, do so on a temporary basis. This indicates that seasonal work is a complement to family labour during periods in which labour availability within the household is below the labour requirements of the farm. Evidently, the need for additional labour is related not only to the size, age, and sex composition of the household (a function of the family's life cycle), but also to crop requirements, amount of available land, and working capital. In Bajo Piura, therefore, a clear relationship exists between cultivated area and use of paid labour: 92% of farms over 2.5 ha hire seasonal workers, mainly during the cotton harvest, whereas only 23% of the farms under 0.5 ha do so (Table 3). In the Altiplano, the association is weaker: 19% of the farms below 1 ha hire seasonal workers, and 32% of those over 4 ha also have temporary labourers, suggesting that seasonal workers function as a substitute for family labour in any area characterized by high migration rates of family dependants.

Another, more theoretical, aspect of economic strategies of poor rural households is the notion of "self-exploitation," first suggested by Chayanov (1974) with regard to the Russian peasantry. A reinterpretation of this concept by Latin American scholars has sought to link it with the Marxian notion of absolute surplus value in contexts where formal subordination of labour to capital predominates (Bartra 1975; Bengoa 1979). These scholars argue that peasant production channeled to the market involves the transfer of variable but significant amounts of unpaid labour because peasant farms face low labour productivity and prices do not cover the total labour input. In other words, should peasant labour (including that of the family members) be valued at market prices, and the prevailing profit rate deducted from total sale price, the peasant unit would face a deficit or a very low rate of return.

To test this complex theory with the survey data, some simple calculations were made. First, the actual monetary income of the family was compared with the estimated wage income these same families would get if all family members who earned income were to receive this regional wage (using data on the prevailing regional rural wage). Our estimates showed that, on average, real family income is greater than income generated from wage labour. Nevertheless, 38% of families in Bajo Piura and 27% in the Altiplano had lower monetary incomes than they would have had if all working members, *excluding* unpaid family labourers, were fully employed and earning the minimum regional rural wage. Surprisingly, these proportions were only slightly lower in the more-developed valleys (around 24% in Cañete and around 26% in Tambopata). This suggests that between 25 and 33% of rural households "self-exploit" their labour force because no alternative, more productive employment is available. It also suggests that absolute poverty characterizes a large proportion of peasant families, regardless of the level of regional development.

The second calculation involved estimating the total family income by multiplying the total number of members working within the households, *including* unpaid family workers, by the regional rural wage, and then comparing this estimate with the real monetary income of the family. Not surprisingly, over 53% of households in Bajo Piura and 56% in the Altiplano had lower real monetary incomes. Thus, the degree of "self-exploitation" apparently increases as more dependants (spouse and children predominantly) work as unpaid family labourers. Although not conclusive, these data provide some evidence in support of the theory of peasant "self-exploitation."

Investment in different alternatives is another economic strategy of rural households. Investment in the farm can be measured indirectly by the use of purchased inputs. Among farms under 1 ha in Bajo Piura, the horse-drawn plow was the most common tool for land preparation (50% of farms), and around 33% used human energy for all agricultural activities. Only about 12% had some kind of mechanical means of land clearing and preparation. Although plows and horses can be rented by the day, most farmers owned theirs. Among farms of 1–5 ha, about 61% used animal energy (mainly the horse-drawn plow), only 13% used human energy exclusively, and mechanical devices predominated on almost 24% of all farms. The majority of farmers also used fertilizers (92%) and pesticides (90%). Thus, farmers in these areas favoured a labour-intensive, intermediate technology that could increase yields per unit area without displacing human labour. Unfortunately, the data do not permit the monetary value of these inputs to be calculated.

In the Altiplano, technological innovation was less noticeable. Only human energy was used for agricultural tasks on 57% of the farms under 1 ha, whereas over 60% of farms of 1–5 ha used animal energy for land preparation. Only 6% of farms under 5 ha used any type of mechanical devices in agriculture. The main inputs were fertilizers, used by over 89% of farms, principally for potatoes. This fertilizer, mainly natural dung that could be obtained from their own cattle or by barter from cattle-raising communities, is also a labour- and land-maximizing technology. In this area, most of the monetary income was invested in children's education and in consumption, because returns on agricultural investments were very low.

SOCIOCULTURAL STRATEGIES AND CONSEQUENCES

Social strategies were based on the manipulation of social relationships and extrafamilial organizations to best achieve individual or collective goals. These strategies operated at different levels: family, kin network, community, and outside world.

Family structure was frequently the result of specific strategies. The tendency to nuclearization and family fission was prevalent in the Altiplano, especially among the poorer households. The main mechanism leading to nuclearization was the emigration of dependants and a neolocal residential pattern after marriage. The scarcity of land, low productivity, and absence of employment opportunities in the area were the main factors behind this social strategy in the Altiplano of Puno.

In Bajo Piura, by contrast, family extension seemed to be a strategy to reduce the costs of housing and to pool resources for consumption. The extended family (over 58% of all families) mainly comprised elderly parents, their married children, and their offspring. Patrilocal residence after marriage appeared to be the common cultural practice. Case studies showed that maintaining at least one married son within the household was a means of preventing further land fragmentation and functioned also as a security mechanism against old age and infirmity of the parents. A larger family could both hold on to its land and take advantage of the seasonal employment opportunities during the cotton harvest in the large cooperative estates. Cotton is harvested by hand and payment is by the amount harvested, so that all able family members usually participate and thus increase total family earnings. Such seasonal employment opportunities were absent in the Altiplano because most of the land owned by the large estates was used for extensive sheep grazing.

Social change in the two more-developed valleys could be characterized as the transformation of peasants into farmers. This process was clear in Cañete, and more complex in Tambopata, the main difference being the absence of stable wage relations in the colonization zones. At this point, it is hard to predict if the colonists of Tambopata will follow the Cañete pattern. Our data showed that migration of dependants for educational reasons, as well as the channeling of capital outside regional agriculture, can stifle capitalist development and the emergence of the capitalist farmer. The stagnation of commercial farming in tropical colonization zones, as a result of inadequate land management, diminishing productivity, and price fluctuations, has been documented elsewhere. Stearman (1978) has termed this process the *barbecho* crisis in relation to Andean colonists in Bolivia. A classical study in this respect is Geertz' (1963) research on agricultural involution in Indonesia. A similar pattern might develop in Tambopata; only time will tell.

Social strategies seemed to be related to family composition in Cañete, where over 51% of households were extended in structure. Most of these families included a subordinated nuclear family, generally a son with his own wife and children. This pattern of extended lineal families provided more domestic labour, and the increased dependency of family members could be coped with because of the relative prosperity of such families in Cañete. Because of the younger ages in most colonists' families in Tambopata, only 20% were extended, with similar structures to those in Cañete: an older couple with married dependants.

Migration is a very important strategy with major social implications in the poor regions. In Puno, migration was a highly structured endeavour that depended on family and kin relations to minimize the risk and costs of uprooting, both economic and emotional. For example, 75% of permanent emigrants from the Altiplano obtained their information on the receiving area from friends, relatives, or neighbours who had already migrated. About 50% actually moved in the company of other household members or close relatives. Also, over 66% had relatives or acquaintances in the place to which they migrated, and most received help from them, especially lodging and food. According to a recent survey of migrants in Lima (Aramburú and Ponce 1985), most migrants also

99

mentioned the help of their relatives and acquaintances in describing their search for work.

Many migrants sent money and presents home, especially those who managed to secure a job. The amount of these remittances was not significant, and mainly served to maintain links with parents and relatives. This strategy is important as a mechanism permitting migrants to return home and still have access to land and housing, should the urban pursuit of a job fail (Altamirano 1984).

The consequence of increasing dependence on external sources of income is a complex process of semiproletarianization that affects almost all of the households of the Altiplano, and those of the middle and lower strata in Bajo Piura. The products of the land are not enough to survive, so temporary jobs must be secured elsewhere. Peasants can work during harvest in their own plot and as wage labourers later during the year, either on a coffee farm of Tambopata or on a large rice estate on the coast. Thus, they are neither real proletarians nor traditional peasants, but are best described as semiproletarians (or semipeasants, depending on what one chooses to emphasize). An orthodox Marxist would probably argue that this is a transitory situation, but these patterns have existed in rural Peru for at least 50 years and, if we believe recent data, the recent economic crisis merely reinforces them.

In spite of this ambiguous situation, the political expression of the rural poor in the Altiplano, as well as in Bajo Piura, has been characterized historically by violent, localized peasant revolts. In the Altiplano, peasant revolts have been numerous and bloody since 1867 and focused upon land rights. Unequal land distribution has persisted, as have the peasants' efforts to obtain direct access to the property of estates that were ancestrally their own. Widespread terrorist activities since 1981, especially in the Southern Andes, have reduced the political alternatives for peasants, because they tend to be thought of as terrorists if they are politically active. Even worse is pressure from terrorist groups demanding support from the peasants and taking drastic measures, including torture and death, if such support is denied. Many peasant leaders have been murdered and their property destroyed in the past 4 years by the terrorist group "Shining Path," of a Marxist/Maoist ideology. Politically overt strategies in this context are therefore losing effectiveness for the peasantry.

The move toward commercial farming also increased the peasants' political awareness and organization. Smallholders in Cañete have a long tradition of defending themselves against the expansion of the hacienda. Today, several agencies work in the area with small-scale farmers, providing extension and credit services. Politically, these farmers are conservative and see the presence of a growing landless peasantry, unable to find employment in the rural cooperatives, as the main threat to their holdings. No strong political organization of medium- and small-scale farmers now exists in the valley.

Political and economic organizations are notoriously lacking in Tambopata, perhaps as a result of dispersed residence patterns and the heterogeneity of origins. The common enemies for the colonist are the service cooperative that monopolizes the marketing of coffee and the state Agrarian

Bank that controls credit. Farms deal with these institutions on an individual basis and lack any form of solid organization.

A final dimension of household strategies concerns educational and economic expectations for children. Most households gave priority to formal education, especially for males. Any available income was used to support students away from home in the best available educational opportunities. Peasants of Bajo Piura sent their children to the high schools of either the main city, Piura, or the next best choice, the regional towns. In the Altiplano, many went all the way to Juliaca, the major commercial city of the area, and had to pay for lodging and food. The wealthier families sent their older children to the regional or national universities of Arequipa and Lima, an important source of pride for the parents. Education was perceived as the surest way to escape poverty and avoid returning to the land. Thus, expectations were placed outside agriculture and the peasant way of life. This strategy was confirmed by the fact that most permanent migrants were young sons and daughters who left their parents' homes as soon as they had completed their secondary education. Although pursuing their education was the main reason for moving, most of them also had to work to pay for their maintenance in the cities.

In the more-developed zones, expectations regarding children are heavily oriented toward specialized technical education in agricultural subjects (Cañete), and on diversification toward trade and transport (Tambopata). In fact, many farmers in Cañete worked with their children who had obtained some type of technical training in agriculture; they were a source of constant innovation and modernization of productive activities on the farm.

Peasants were asked if they felt they could improve their agricultural productivity. Answers varied, but among the least educated, a common attitude was to "blame nature." Specifically, this outlook placed the responsibility for poor agricultural performance on factors such as too much or too little rain, poor soils, and climatic changes. Evidently, the farmer could do little to prevent these natural phenomena except to pray and hope for the best. Peasants in Cañete and Tambopata, by contrast, were more likely to blame the government for economic and other problems.

Ironically, after the end of the fieldwork in 1979, both Puno and Bajo Piura suffered major natural disasters. Since 1981, the Altiplano has had the worst drought in decades, lasting until the summer of 1984 when heavy rains, a sequel of the El Niño phenomenon, produced excessive rainfall and severe flooding. In Bajo Piura, heavy rains caused the worst floods in a century during the first months of 1983, with severe losses to housing and crops.

POLICY IMPLICATIONS

Some suggestions on rural development policies can be based on the findings from this study. The main and obvious conclusion is that the heterogeneity of regional development patterns requires specific regional policies for rural development, because no single approach will be valid in every case. Decision-making should be flexible and decentralized and local human resources should be used to design and develop particular programs for rural development in each area.

More specifically, in areas such as Cañete and most of the central coast, extension services, credit facilities, and the lateral diffusion of innovations need to be improved. These improvements could best be achieved by establishing production committees of farms with similar crop mix and increasing institutional facilities to permit the exchange of experience among farmers. Experimentation with, and diffusion of, labour-intensive and land-saving technologies is also advisable, in response to the increasing demand for foodstuffs for nearby urban markets.

Parcelization of the rural cooperative lands, although seen as an immediate solution to demographic and political pressure, severely fragments land holdings. Land titling offices should regulate this and encourage land consolidation. Subsidies to foster food production could be given through cheaper inputs, instead of raising prices through imperfect marketing mechanisms. Security of tenure should be guaranteed for small and medium farms (over 1 ha and less than 15 ha) to promote capital investment in land improvements.

Finally, seasonal workers should be organized to manage demand and supply of labour in a more rational manner, and to guarantee some participation in social and indirect benefits. Tax systems could be designed on a fixed rate per area and not as a proportion of total income that diminishes profits as land productivity increases.

In the colonization zones of Puno, as well as in many tropical colonization areas of South America, a major concern should be land and water management and conservation. Deforestation of steep slopes is producing an increasingly serious problem of land degradation through erosion, leaching, and soil compaction. As demographic pressure increases in the nearby Andean zones, new colonists arrive in the valley and settle on steep terrain that is inadequate for agricultural purposes. In the long run, this process can jeopardize the agricultural potential of the whole valley. Programs to control and plan new settlements, to promote reforestation, and to introduce simple technologies of land and water conservation, such as terracing and gulley control, are required.

Another issue concerns increasing land productivity. Because most farmers use little modern technology for coffee cultivation, better crop management, pest control, and improved varieties could certainly increase yields per unit area. Nevertheless, the adoption of these inputs requires economic incentives for on-farm investment, such as better prices, cheaper credit, and a more competitive marketing system. Increased productivity would also reduce wasteful expansion of the agricultural frontier, and create less abandoned land and more employment per cultivated area. As the population grows and stabilizes, demand for foodstuffs, which are now largely imported into the region, will increase. Therefore, the production of food crops for local consumption should also be considered. Finally, land titling should be increased because insecurity of tenure now prevents more permanent investments on the farm.

Policy alternatives for the depressed areas are much harder to define and implement because these involve major political decisions at the highest level of government. In Bajo Piura, it will be hard to prevent further land fragmentation because of demographic pressure and the absence of alternative employment opportunities in the region. A short-term alternative could be diversifying the sources of credit to include crafts and crop processing. Because the flatness of the valley and high evaporation is causing salinization problems in about 33% of the agricultural land, better water management is crucial, as well as improvement in the drainage system for small farms. More land- and labour-intensive technology, such as associated cultivation, should be promoted through improved extension services. Peasant organization should be supported to take up productive activities in marketing and the provision of inputs. Finally, birth-control programs, tied to basic sanitary measures, are also required in this region.

Small-scale farmers of the Altiplano present the greatest challenge to development projects. Lack of land is not an absolute problem because, due to absence of irrigation and artificial fertilizers, about 50% of usable land is under long fallow periods. Intermediate technological packages have to be researched through the improvement of traditional skills and knowledge based on Andean technology. Drought- and cold-resistant varieties of food crops should be tested in the region and, if successful, distributed to the peasant communities. Land redistribution is also a major requirement because the huge ranching cooperatives control about 68% of the arable land and use it extensively. Here also, diversification of productive activities including weaving, tourism, pottery, fishing, and rearing small animals (especially guinea pigs, which are a staple and major source of protein in the Andean diet) should be promoted through credit and training.

Land and water management are also crucial issues in the Altiplano. Because most agriculture is rain-fed, water conservation is of central importance. An annual average rainfall of 800 mm is barely sufficient for agriculture; hence, alternative means of irrigation should be promoted through the creation of reservoirs and small irrigation projects. Erosion and overgrazing are critical problems in the upper zones and where the topography is irregular. Poor pastures and intensive slope cultivation have turned most of the broken terrain into wasteland, and these areas should be restored by reforestation, herd and pasture management, and soil conservation. In the last century, livestock breeding and ranching have been heavily emphasized, as well as sheep and cattle rearing, displacing the native South American herds (alpacas and llamas) to poorer pastures and less capitalized units of production. Great potential exists in the international market for natural fibres, and clothing made from alpaca and mixed fibres, provided that productivity is improved and breeding problems are overcome. More technical research and extension are required to enable Andean herders to improve the management and genetic quality of their flocks. Finally, supporting programs such as maternal and child health care, family planning, nutritional extension, sanitation, and technical education should be included in rural development planning for this region.

Perhaps the principal consideration should be to increase the political visibility and importance of small-scale farmers, especially in the Andes. In the long run, this is a task that only they themselves, through their political organizations, can accomplish.

Appendix 1. Model of household strategies in rural stagnant zones.[a]

External factors	Household strategies	Internal factors
Ecological limitations to expanding agricultural productivity: temperature, climate, altitude (A); low rainfall, poor availability of water, poor drainage (BP)	*Demographic* Marriage delay, abortion (A) Permanent expulsion of dependants for economic reasons	Small (A) or large families (BP) High fertility (BP) or low fertility and high infant mortality (A) Low masculinity index
Poor soils Stagnant agricultural frontier Land concentration	Seasonal migration of male adults for temporary jobs: long distance (A), short distance (BP) *Economic*	High (A) or low (BP) age at marriage Older families High permanent and seasonal mobility
Capital-intensive innovations (BP); extensive use of pastures (A)	Crop and on-farm diversification: cash and food (BP), consumption (A)	Minifundio Fragmentation (A)
Capitalist expansion is market oriented but not market dominated	Job diversification: wage (BP), self-employed (A) Seasonal wage labour used as complement for unpaid family labour (BP)	Few technological innovations: low yields; low labour productivity Dual-purpose production: consumption and sale
Social relations of production based on *huaccha* system (A), or seasonal workers (BP)	Increasing "self-exploitation" to cope with adverse conditions (A)	Low levels of capital accumulation, little or no capital investment in agriculture
Few employment opportunities in agricultural or industrial sector	*Social–cultural* Family fission (A) or extension to cope with increasing consumption costs (housing) (BP)	Low educational levels (BP) Nuclear (A) or extended *refugio* (BP) family structure
Rapid natural growth of population, low growth rate due to outmigration	Increasing dependence on external sources of income: local (BP), extraregional (A)	Low living standards Little social differentiation
Negative terms of trade; adverse price policy	Semiproletarianization and land invasions and violence "Blame nature" outlook Expectations for children outside agriculture and family business	

[a] Altiplano Puno (A) and Bajo Piura (BP).

Appendix 2. Model of household strategies in rural developing zones.[a]

External factors	Household strategies	Internal factors
Favourable ecology: stable climate (C); more rainfall and favourable climate (T)	*Demographic*	Larger families
Good soils (C); good initial soil fertility (T)	Birth control (C)[b]	Medium (T) to low (C) fertility
Expanding agricultural frontier: irrigation projects (C) and colonization (T)	Temporary (C) or permanent (T) outmigration of dependants for education	Low mortality (C)
Less land concentration: medium cooperatives (C) and no haciendas (T)	No or little seasonal migration of household heads	High masculinity index
Labour-intensive innovations (C); more profitable cash crops, coffee (T)	*Economic*	Younger (T) or older (C) families
Capitalist expansion is market dominated	Crop specialization (T), double cropping (C)	Low permanent and seasonal mobility
Social relations of production based on intensive use of family labour, and permanent and seasonal wage labour (C) and seasonal wage labour (T)	Increasing technical innovations for higher land productivity (C)	Medium farms
Expanding employment opportunities in agricultural sector	Use of wage labour as complement of family labour (T); permanent wage labourers as substitute of family labour (C)	Nucleated property
Rapid population growth through immigration	Main source of income is farm production, profits reinvested on farm (C) or related activities (T)	Technological innovations (inputs and new crops)
	Social–cultural	Predominance of cash crops
	From peasants to farmers	Significant levels of capital accumulation; reinvestment of profits on farm (C); land purchases (T)
	Family extension to provide labour force	Higher educational levels (C)
	Institutional pressure for better prices	Extended lineal family structure (C)
	"Blame the government" outlook	High living standards
	Expectations for children in farm (C) and in trade (T)	High social differentiation

[a] Cañete (C) and tropical Puno (Tambopata, T).
[b] From indirect evidence (i.e., not from survey data).

PART 2

CONCLUSIONS

Impact of Development on Household Demographic Behaviour

Carol Vlassoff

This concluding chapter attempts to draw together the most important common insights from the previous studies. It begins with some general observations concerning "survival strategies," a theme that permeates many of the studies. The subsequent section examines what has been learned concerning the economic, demographic, and social effects of development on rural households.

Demographic Behaviour as Survival Strategies

The studies are all concerned, to a large extent, with changing economic conditions and the subsequent demographic and social adjustments. Many of the papers use the term "survival strategies" to describe these processes. Because this concept has been seriously questioned (Vlassoff 1983), a few remarks on the value of this approach in the context of demographic analysis seem relevant.

The survival strategies theme is becoming increasingly prevalent in demographic literature and is found in many of the contributions in this volume. The concept was first used by Duque and Pastrana (1973) in their analysis of the economic activities of poor families in Santiago, Chile. The authors referred to an "objective strategy for economic subsistence" that was not necessarily conscious for those undertaking it.

From purely economic beginnings, the concept has been transformed by demographers to include biological reproduction and to make economic behaviour (or "material reproduction") dependent upon demographic phenomena (Torrado 1981). The problem with this approach is that it implies that high fertility and migration are rational and calculated strategies designed to ensure the survival of poor Third World families. For example Arizpe (1981) described the survival strategy of "relay migration," a process whereby rural Mexican families sent their members, in

109

progressive order, to urban areas to work. The cash remittances from migrating members provided financial support to their families and contributed to rural production and welfare. She suggests that (but does not explain why) four or more children are required to ensure a family's "minimum social reproduction" and to allow it to avail itself of the strategy of relay migration.

On the other hand, it can also be argued that peasants resort to migration to sustain the livelihood of their large families rather than as part of a predetermined plan in which fertility and migration decisions are interrelated. In many of the papers in this volume, migration seemed to be more of an "after the fact" adjustment to poor economic circumstances (Aramburú, Forni and Benencia, Giraldo, Hackenberg, and Ong). Bhattacharyya's account of labouring children in the ornament-making industry also argued against the view that high fertility is a calculated strategy to maximize family welfare.

On the other hand, poor rural families seem to adopt various demographic strategies, not merely to survive, but to improve their economic conditions as much as possible. That such wealth optimization may be a strategy for risk alleviation by rural families has been emphasized by Stark (1981), and many chapters in this volume also substantiate this viewpoint (Aramburú, Forni and Benencia, Hackenberg, and Ong). Gomes (1984) also found that Kenyan parents viewed fertility as a means of ensuring economic betterment through the outmigration of, and remittances received from, educated children.

In short, then, the concept of survival strategies is confusing in that it implies that fertility and migration represent consciously planned behaviour designed to ensure a minimum level of economic subsistence. In fact, the strategies described in much of the literature are primarily economic in nature — poverty-reducing or risk-aversion devices. Hence, the term seems most appropriate if limited to economic applications only. In the papers that appear here, the concept of survival strategies is, in fact, used to refer mainly to economic strategies, although several authors apply it less precisely to demographic behaviour as well (e.g., Aramburú and Ong). Even these authors, however, use the term in a loosely metaphorical sense and, in any case, the main findings of the studies are not contingent upon a strict definition of this concept.

ECONOMIC DIVERSIFICATION

The studies have focused, for the most part, on the impact of modernizing forces, such as new technology and agrarian reform, on agricultural development, rural institutions, and demographic and social behaviour. These studies provide a rich body of descriptive information on rural communities and families and their adjustments to changing economic circumstances. In some cases, these circumstances have improved for most peasant families as a result of progressive and effective policies;

110

in others, they have deteriorated through implemented policies that benefit only a handful of wealthy farmers.

Perhaps the most important conclusion, common to all the studies, is that the responses of peasant families to modernization are varied, complex, and adaptive. Hence, single theoretical models or broad generalizations are unable to explain the complexity of rural adaptation to modernizing influences in contemporary Third World societies. In particular, the polarization hypothesis (discussed explicitly by Hackenberg and implicitly by others) has been shown to be inadequate to encompass the innovative ways in which families reacted to changing conditions and opportunities.

Hackenberg shows how the Green Revolution led to *diversification* of employment and cropping patterns in the Digos-Padada Valley of the Philippines. The breaking of landlord–tenant bonds by land reform and the provision of credit to the small-scale farmer transformed traditional agricultural structures and expanded business and employment opportunities in rural areas. In Malaysia, too, industrial development led to significant changes in rural subsistence patterns and diversified roles for rural men and women. In Sreebollobpur, the Bangladesh Academy for Rural Development (BARD) program diversified cropping and occupational patterns, including a much higher participation of women in the rural labour force than elsewhere in Bangladesh. Aramburú discusses the process of *structural heterogeneity* in Cañete, Peru, which is similar to Hackenberg's description of diversification. Peasants were transformed into farmers as a result of agricultural development, an equitable system of land distribution, and market opportunities.

However, employment also diversified because of lack of development and fewer economic opportunities. For example, in the Altiplano and Bajo Piura, Peru, diversification incorporated both cash and subsistence crops, more out of necessity than out of economic innovation. Aramburú notes, for example, that poorer households sometimes had to sell crops for cash only to buy them back later in the year. In Argentina and Colombia, too, modernization of agriculture forced poorer families to turn to other kinds of employment, often of a wage-earning or seasonal nature.

These studies have also illustrated considerable resilience and determination among rural families in adjusting to deteriorating social and economic conditions. Wage workers in Argentina, for example, responded to the diminishing demand for labour in the sugar industry by diversifying their productive activities to include work in the construction and service sectors, seasonal migration to other provinces, subsistence farming, and handicraft production. Similar adjustments were made by poor households in the Altiplano and Bajo Piura, Peru, which integrated the migration of family members, both temporary and permanent, with traditional subsistence farming. In the Philippines, tenants removed from their land by landlords fearing agrarian reform took advantage of more profitable alternatives such as contract labour and share and wage arrangements. In Colombia, smallholding farmers, although in many ways more closely tied to the land than landowners or sharecroppers, turned to other nonagricultural activities such as personal services and other trades to make ends meet.

A finding common to several of the studies (Aramburú, Forni and Benencia, Giraldo, and Ong) is that a substantial proportion of peasant families uses unpaid family labour to increase household income but these family workers often earn less than they would from wage labour. This tends to support Chayanov's (1974) concept of the "self-exploitation" of poor rural households, at least among the poorest peasant classes, discussed in previous chapters. Chayanov, however, in demonstrating such self-exploitation, was attempting to argue for the existence of a peasant economy that cannot be explained by classical economic theory. For peasants, he argued, the objective of family labour is not profit, but rather the satisfaction of subsistence needs. Chayanov did not contend, as many Latin American authors do, that peasants self-exploit because of poverty and lack of other options. Hence, as Heynig (1982) has convincingly argued, the applicability of Chayanov's theory to the Latin American situation is questionable.

Aramburú's evidence that economic self-exploitation increased as more family members worked as unpaid labourers is also interesting, and deserves further exploration. Can we deduce, for example, that higher fertility leads to greater self-exploitation or is the practice only apparent in areas where high unemployment and poor economic conditions prevail? Future research may throw further light on these questions.

DEMOGRAPHIC RESPONSES TO DEVELOPMENT

In several of the case studies, samples are rather small to draw definitive conclusions concerning the relationship between economic development and fertility decline. Moreover, in two studies (India and Peru), the number of surviving children is used to measure fertility, but it is not a true proxy because the effects of child mortality are ignored. Assuming that fertility levels are captured fairly accurately in these studies, however, we may conclude that the generally observed relationship between economic development and declining fertility was found to be true in most of the cases cited.

In Bangladesh, for example, fertility was much lower in the study area than in the country as a whole and, among wealthier families in Argentina, fertility was considerably lower than among wage workers. In rural Colombia, similar patterns were observed, with the higher-income families in all sectors having fewer children than poorer ones. Declining fertility could also be predicted in Malaysia where young unmarried women in the free trade zones wanted no more than four children, in contrast to an average completed family size of over six children among the older women. Adoption of family planning was also a response to favourable social and economic circumstances in the rural Philippines. In Peru, too, fertility was inversely related to economic status in each of the four regions studied, although in the poor Altiplano, fertility was surprisingly low, due to practices such as late marriage and a high incidence of abortion.

The relationship between fertility and the economic value of children was not, however, consistent across the various studies. In Argentina, a large number of children and, hence, a large family labour force, helped to ensure economic survival among the wage-earning peasants. In the Altiplano of Peru, on the other hand, conditions were so poor, and opportunities for employment so limited, that children were more of a drain on family resources than an economic asset; hence, family size was lower than in the more prosperous regions of the country. In Bangladesh, peasants viewed the education of children and the resulting employment opportunities as a means to obtain increased security and status: large numbers of children were incompatible with these objectives. Farmers in the Philippines also placed a high premium on the education of children, and land reform precluded the support of large numbers of offspring on existing plots.

The study most directly concerned with the relationship between the economic value of children and fertility is that of Bhattacharyya and Hayes, in which children's labour was not only observed but measured quantitatively. The labour of children was found to be a result, rather than a cause, of high fertility. The income that children made was not an incentive for parents to have more children; rather, they expressed shame at sending their children to work and would have preferred to see them in school. Hence, the small amount of income that children can earn in societies that are modernizing may be insufficient to motivate high fertility. Child labour, at least in the present studies, seems to have been more a response to poor economic conditions than a deliberate strategy for maximizing family welfare.

Another factor that continues to play a role in the determination of family size is son preference. This was indicated in the study by Forni and Benencia, where the sex ratio at birth was skewed in favour of sons. Son preference was also apparent in Sreebollobpur. However, there was some evidence that, with increasing modernization, girls are valued, if not more than boys, at least more than previously. In the Philippines, for example, girls were delaying marriage and staying in school longer; simultaneously, labour force participation of women in all sectors of the economy was increasing. In Malaysia, daughters made a significant contribution to household budgets and were valued more than sons, at least from an economic standpoint. Sons, it was found, often disappointed their parents by not sharing their earnings with their families after they had obtained jobs outside the village. Findings such as these deserve more attention as they could have important policy implications.

As noted, economic development was accompanied, in most studies, by a rising age at marriage, especially among females. Later marriage was generally linked to lower fertility, such as in the Philippines and Bangladesh. However, evidence to the contrary was found among wage workers in the dry area of Argentina who, in spite of late marriage, had just as many children as their counterparts in the irrigated area who married much younger.

Contraceptive use is also clearly on the increase, and was especially notable in Bangladesh, rural Colombia, Malaysia, and the Philippines.

Unfortunately, the studies did not provide much information on contraceptive choice or on patterns of contraceptive use. In Bangladesh and the Philippines, modern contraceptive methods were promoted by family-planning programs and apparently used effectively in the study areas. In Latin America, the information is sketchy, but traditional methods seem to play an important role. Although some evidence of artificial contraception was also found in the Latin American studies, less attention was devoted to this phenomenon in the research and, hence, the conclusions remain tentative.

Migration was shown to be an important response to differing levels of economic development. The nature and implications of migration strategies seemed to vary according to regional characteristics and labour force opportunities, broadly reflecting a push–pull pattern. All studies showed a tendency for those areas experiencing favourable economic trends, such as the rural Philippines and the more prosperous settlements in Argentina, Colombia, and Peru, to retain population to a considerable extent. This indicates that rural development and effective agrarian policies can stabilize rural communities positively, an important finding for regions, such as Latin America, where heavy rural-to-urban migration is a serious problem. These studies show that employment opportunities in the agricultural sector make the countryside a more attractive destination than is generally supposed. It is notable that migrating children generally kept close ties with their families of origin, facilitating easy reentry into their communities should this become necessary or desirable in later years. Interestingly, these ties were significant more from an emotional than an economic point of view because their monetary value, at least in the Peruvian case, was relatively small.

Various migration patterns were witnessed in the studies, particularly in Argentina, Colombia, Peru, and the Philippines. In Peru, for example, migration was infrequent in the more-developed areas. Immigration, on the other hand, was prevalent in response to job opportunities and general economic growth. The stagnant economic areas, by contrast, were characterized by widespread migration, both permanent and seasonal. In the unirrigated area of Argentina, seasonal migration, combined with economic diversification, allowed families to survive in precarious economic conditions. Migration from the more prosperous settlers' community in the irrigated zone was predominantly of children to urban areas. Migration of families in the traditional capitalist sector of Colombia was also mainly of this type. This seemed to be related not only to pull factors, including the financial capacity of these families to send children to school, but also to push factors including population density and small plot sizes.

For similar reasons, considerable outmigration occurred in the Philippines, especially among the younger labour force cohorts. It is difficult, then, to generalize concerning the relationship between migration and economic development in rural societies in the process of modernization: a variety of economic, demographic, and social considerations clearly influences migration strategies. Microlevel studies, such as the ones described here, are therefore indispensable in interpreting these interrelationships within particular contexts.

SOCIAL RESPONSES TO DEVELOPMENT

The social adjustments made by families to different economic circumstances is highlighted by several studies. For example, the general socioeconomic status of the household was often reflected in its structure and composition. The degree to which this was a deliberate or premeditated response is an open question but the final outcome, in most cases, were families whose members contributed to household welfare in ways that were inherently rational from an economic standpoint. As in the case of demographic responses to varying economic circumstances, specific family responses are difficult to predict and interpret in the absence of microlevel observation of prevailing conditions. In general, however, families are becoming more nuclear although not necessarily because of improved economic circumstances.

In Peru, for example, opposite family strategies were adopted in the two stagnant areas, although levels of living per se were fairly similar. In the Altiplano, nuclear families were common because productive land and job opportunities were scarce. In Bajo Piura, on the other hand, the extended family was the strategy adopted to reduce housing costs and to pool resources. In Argentina, nuclear families predominated in all areas but were most prevalent among the wealthiest peasants whose economic security did not depend upon a large number of family members. Wage workers, by contrast, were characterized by a much higher proportion of extended families (although, even here, nuclear arrangements still prevailed in most families) in which members pooled their resources to ensure household subsistence. In Malaysia, modernization had entailed the outmigration of children to work in the modern sector; hence, the trend toward nuclear families was also increasing.

All studies shared the universal findings that peasant families value education highly. Although the reasons for which it was sought varied according to particular economic and environmental circumstances, it was generally seen as the means to greater economic security. In some cases, as in the stagnant areas of Peru, education was directed toward higher studies and nonagricultural pursuits; in the more progressive zones of Cañete and Tambopata, specialized technical training was more popular. Education was seen, therefore, as a means of both changing unfavourable economic conditions and of improving already favourable circumstances. The latter was the case, as well, in Argentina, Bangladesh, Colombia, India, Malaysia, and the Philippines.

Although most of the studies were not primarily concerned with the impact of modernization on women's roles, many indicated that important changes were occurring in women's activities and, indirectly, in their status. These changes were especially marked in the Malaysian free trade zones. Unmarried daughters had become the mainstay of "the physical and social subsistence of the rural system" in terms of their contributions to the domestic economy. The wage labour of young women was directly related to postponement of marriage because, as the major wage earners, they were required to help with the education of siblings and also to accumulate sufficient savings for a wedding. Their freedom to leave home also was dependent on their potential replacement by a wage-earning sibling. Thus, the possibility of wage employment created a considerable burden on these young women, and converted traditional roles of dependence into ones of heavy responsibility. Conflicts of values were also experienced, particularly in relation to sexual behaviour, counterbalanced by a pronounced reassertion of Islamic fundamentalism in many of the modern factories. Hence, the response of such women to the modern work environment seems to be one of role conflict, a complex mix of old and new values. On the one hand, they display modern attitudes to economic independence, marriage, child-bearing, and divorce, yet they observe strict Islamic customs in the workplace, including adopting Middle Eastern dress and rigidly segregating the sexes.

In the rural Philippines, too, women entered gainful employment at astonishing rates as a result of the diversification of economic opportunities. This increase was especially apparent in the area of small business, in both agricultural and nonagricultural sectors. Although Hackenberg does not link these changes directly to changes in women's status, he does note their relationship to higher ages at marriage and lower fertility, which indirectly reflect a rising female status. In Bangladesh, the education of daughters was becoming more valued, not so much as a reflection of the increased status of women, but rather because prospects for marriage were thereby improved. Nonetheless, education is an important first step in raising women's self-consciousness and awareness of inequalities.

In the Latin American papers, women were becoming increasingly involved in paid agricultural labour and in the diversification of employment. This was largely a response to economic necessity, and the degree to which it represents modern attitudes and behaviour is questionable. It seems that here, in contrast to the Asian cases, sufficient incentives for lucrative nonfamilial employment were not available to permit women to advance themselves, basic subsistence being their principal preoccupation.

CONTRIBUTIONS OF THE MICROAPPROACH

Finally, a few conclusions may be drawn concerning the value of the microapproach to studies on the impact of development on household behaviour. All studies had the advantage of complementing quantitative surveys with in-depth observation of local institutions, social and economic structures, and traditional bonds and relationships over several months. This gave the analyses both richness and depth in the interpretation of survey results that would not have been possible through the survey approach alone. Several of the authors (Aramburú, Hackenberg, and Ong) are anthropologists, whereas the others are social scientists who complemented their survey research with residence in the selected communities to observe and interpret rural behaviour.

Hackenberg reports changes over a 10-year period, during which he spent considerable time in the region observing socioeconomic and political changes. This provided vital information for interpreting unexpected results of the longitudinal study, i.e., that the hypothesized fertility differences between the two rural areas did not result. Whereas it was expected that the more-developed area, Magsaysay, would advance more quickly with regard to economic indicators and family planning, the opposite occurred. Peasant families in Matanao, the more disadvantaged community, dramatically altered their cropping patterns to take advantage of agrarian reform rather than allowing themselves to stagnate under traditional productive arrangements. The dramatic changes brought about by land reform gave Matanao farmers new opportunities and, although considerable adjustments were necessary to take advantage of these possibilities, cultivators willingly began to shift from corn to rice farming. Failing to grasp these microlevel contextual factors, the researcher would have been hard pressed to explain why fertility declined to almost identical levels in the depressed and more-developed regions of Matanao and Magsaysay. In other words, two surveys alone, without the benefit of anthropological insights, could have led the researcher to conclude that development inputs had had no apparent impact on demographic behaviour because both communities showed similar changes in the dependent variables (such as family planning, fertility, and age at marriage).

Bhattacharyya and Hayes were able to provide greater understanding of the motivation for child labour, and parents' perceptions of it, as a result of Bhattacharyya's residence in the community over the months of data collection. The observation that parents experienced a sense of shame at having to send their children to work is an example of the kind of insight gained through the microapproach. Similarly, Ong's interpretation of the phenomenon of increasing Islamization among young female factory workers in Malaysia has added weight because it is based on continuous contact with these women over the study period.

Several negative consequences resulting from development activities were also emphasized by the microapproach. For example, Bhattacharyya and Hayes' study of the economic value of children yielded important insights into the deterioration of the quality of life of families engaged in the industry. They caution that further research is needed before policies that encourage the expansion of cottage and agroindustries as a means to Third World economic development are widely endorsed. Ong's study showed that young women's circumstances had also deteriorated in certain ways, even though they had been introduced to modern technology and new values. They were now assuming double workloads as well as increasing responsibility for their families. Hence, it is unreasonable to expect that exposure to modern technology is sufficient to improve the quality of life, unless it is accompanied by other changes in gender roles and family-support arrangements. Although such negative results may be only temporary, reflecting perhaps a threshold stage between traditional practices and the abandonment of such patterns for modern lifestyles, policies need to be sensitive to the difficulties of these transitions.

Based on in-depth study of particular communities or microregions, important policy recommendations were also derived from some of the studies. In Peru, Aramburú identified significant policy alternatives for alleviating the problems of the depressed and more-advanced zones. For example, he noted that the traditional South American llama and alpaca herds had been largely displaced by sheep and cattle in the Altiplano, a very depressed region. Because of the large potential demand for the natural fibres from these native animals, research to improve the quality and quantity of these herds was recommended.

In the Philippines, Hackenberg demonstrated that openness to change along one dimension (agricultural innovation) was important for determining willingness to undertake birth-control measures. He also showed how energetic government programs can complement one another in providing a range of options to people in a transition phase, as well as adequate information and communication. Similarly, in Bangladesh, rural families responded favourably to the agricultural, economic, and social opportunities provided by the BARD scheme. The study cited by Khuda reflects significant changes in attitudes and behaviour within single generations.

CONCLUSION

In spite of the important contributions of the papers in this volume to the relationship between socioeconomic development and demographic change, many questions remain unanswered. The most important of these is the degree to which demographic change was attributable strictly to the particular development program taking place in the regions under study, as opposed to what would have occurred without such activities. Hackenberg's study used a methodology that should have yielded this kind of answer in that a longitudinal study was undertaken, with baseline data as well as "experimental" and "control" areas. Because of unexpected changes in the control area, however, the expected differences did not emerge. In the Bangladesh study, comparisons were possible between the "experimental" area, Comilla, and the nation as a whole. The latter, however, cannot strictly be considered a control because it comprises all regions of the country, and the statistics that emerge are national averages, of which Comilla is also a part. In Argentina, Colombia, and Peru, the impact of development was measured even less exactly, by comparing different regions, economic groups, and occupations that were affected differently, or not at all, by modernizing influences.

The search for more reliable controls in cross-sectional and longitudinal impact studies raises the often-cited difficulty of assuming that any human behaviour, especially that of social groups, will remain constant during the experiment or survey. Moreover, the development activities under study may not proceed in the expected manner or the population exposed to such activities may react quite differently than expected. Hence, placing too much weight on the results of such studies may also be problematic. Therefore, a combination of methodological approaches, such as that used in the Philippines study, may be the most appropriate for investigating the impact of development activities on demographic behaviour. Such a combination of longitudinal and quasi-experimental designs, quantitative surveys, and microlevel observation allows the researcher considerable flexibility in selecting the positive contributions of each method, and in compensating for the inevitable deficiencies created by the nature of the data with which social scientists must work.

REFERENCES

Altamirano, T. 1984. Migración de retorno a los Andes. Instituto Andino de Estudios en Población y Desarrollo, Lima, Peru.

Anonymous. 1979. Editorial. The Sunday Mail, 2 December 1979.

Aramburú, C. 1982. Las migraciones en la economía campesina: el caso de Puno. Revista Economía (Universidad Católica del Perú, Lima, Peru), 5(10), 85–102.

Aramburú, C., Ponce, A. 1983. Familia y trabajo en el Perú rural. Instituto Andino de Estudios en Población y Desarrollo, Lima, Peru.

_____. 1985. Estrategias de sobrevivencia entre los sectores populares de Lima. Instituto Andino de Estudios en Población y Desarrollo, Lima, Peru.

Argentina, Government of. 1914, 1947, 1960, 1970, 1980. National Population Census. Buenos Aires, Argentina.

Ariffin, J. 1980. Industrial development in Peninsular Malaysia and rural–urban migration of women workers: impact and implications. Jurnal Ekonomi Malaysia, 1.

Arizpe, L. 1975. Migración por relevos, familia campesina y reproducción social del campesinado. Mexico. Mimeo.

Arizpe, L. 1981. Relay migration and the survival of the peasant household. In Balan, J., ed., Why people move. United Nations Educational Scientific and Cultural Organization, Paris, France.

Bangladesh, Government of. 1978. Bangladesh Fertility Survey, 1975–76. Ministry of Health and Population Control, Dhaka, Bangladesh.

_____. 1981a. Bangladesh Contraceptive Prevalence Survey, 1979. National Institute for Population Research and Training, Dhaka, Bangladesh.

_____. 1981b. Bangladesh Contraceptive Prevalence Survey, 1981. Population Control and Family Planning Division, Dhaka, Bangladesh.

_____. 1983. Statistical yearbook of Bangladesh. Bureau of Statistics, Dhaka, Bangladesh.

_____. 1984. Bangladesh population census, 1981: analytical findings and national tables. Bureau of Statistics, Dhaka, Bangladesh.

_____. 1986. Statistical yearbook of Bangladesh, 1984–85. Bureau of Statistics, Dhaka, Bangladesh.

Barker, R., Cordova, V.G. 1978. Labor utilization in rice production. In Economic consequences of the new rice technology: Proceedings of the Conference on the Economic Consequences of New Rice Technology held at the Institute, Los Baños, 13–16 December 1976. International Rice Research Institute, Los Baños, Philippines. pp.113–136.

Bartra, R. 1975. La teoría del valor y la economía campesina. Revista Comercio Exterior (Banco Nacional de Comercio Exterior, México), 25(5).

Bengoa, J. 1979. Economía campesina y acumulación capitalista. In Plaza, O., ed., La economía campesina. Centro de Estudios y Promoción del Desarrollo, Lima, Peru.

Berquo, E., Loyola, A. 1982. Sobre as estrategias natrimoniaisa presents na sociedade brasilera. Anais do 3 Encontro da Associacao Brasileira de Estudos Populacionais, Rio de Janeiro, Brazil.

Bhattacharyya, A.K. 1982. Impact of cottage industry on fertility: a case study in rural India. Paper presented at 51st Annual Meeting of Population Association of America, San Diego, 29 April–1 May.

Binswanger, H.P., Ruttan, V. 1977. Induced innovation: technology, institutions and development. Johns Hopkins University Press, Baltimore, MD, USA.

Cain, M., Norris, M., Sirageldin, I. 1976. Pre-independence levels of fertility: evidence from the Pakistan National Family Planning Impact Survey, 1968–69. Paper presented at the Bangladesh Fertility Seminar, Cox's Bazaar, Bangladesh.

Caldwell, J.C. 1976. Toward a restatement of demographic transition theory. Population and Development Review, 2(3), 321–366.

_____. 1980. Mass education as a determinant of the timing of fertility decline. Population and Development Review, 6(2), 225–255.

_____. 1982. A theory of fertility decline. Academic Press, New York, NY, USA.

Caldwell, J.C., Reddy, P.H., Caldwell, P. 1982. The determinants of fertility decline in India. Australian National University, Canberra, Australia.

Castillo, G. 1983. How participatory is participatory development? Philippine Institute for Development Studies, Manila, Philippines.

Chayanov, A. 1974. La Organización de la Unidad Económica Campesina. Nueva Visión, Buenos Aires, Argentina.

Chowdhury, K.M., Razzak, A., Becker, S., Sardar, A., D'Souza, S. 1982. Demographic surveillance system, Matlab: Vol. 9 — Vital elements and migration, 1979. International Centre for Diarrhoeal Disease Research (Bangladesh), Dhaka, Bangladesh. Scientific Report 56.

Collins, J. 1983. The maintenance of peasant coffee production in a Peruvian valley. University of New York, Binghamton, NY, USA.

Concepción, M., Smith, P.C. 1977. The demographic situation in the Philippines. East–West Center, Honolulu, HI, USA. Papers of the East–West Population Institute, 44.

de Janvry, A. 1981. The agrarian question and reformism in Latin America. Johns Hopkins University Press, Baltimore, MD, USA.

de Vanzo, J. 1981. Migration and fertility: some illustrative tabulations based on the Malaysian Family Life Survey. Rand Corporation, Santa Monica, CA, USA.

Duff, B. 1978. Mechanization and use of modern varieties. In Economic consequences of the new rice technology: Proceedings of the Conference on the Economic Consequences of New Rice Technology held at the Institute, Los Baños, 13–16 December 1976. International Rice Research Institute, Los Baños, Philippines. pp.165–172.

Duque, J., Pastrana, E. 1973. Las estrategias de supervivencia económica de las unidades familiares del sector popular urbano: una investigación exploratoria. Programa Escuela Latinoamericana de Sociología/Centro Latinoamericano de Demografía, Santiago, Chile.

Easterlin, R.A., ed. 1980. Population and economic change in developing countries. Chicago University Press, Chicago, IL, USA.

Forni, F., Benencia, R. 1983. Evolución del empleo agropecuario en la Argentina 1914–1969. Centro de Estudios e Investigaciones Laborales, Buenos Aires, Argentina.

Forni, F., Aparicio, S., Neiman, G. 1984. Análisis de la estructura ocupacional y los movimientos migratorios en la Provincia de Santiago del Estero, 1970–80. Centro de Estudios e Investigaciones Laborales/Consejo Nacional de Investigaciones Científicas y Técnicas, Buenos Aires, Argentina.

Foster, G. 1965. Peasant society and the image of the limited good. American Anthropologist, 67(4), 293–315.

Gable, R.M., Springer, J.F. 1979. Administrative implications of development policy: comparative analysis of agricultural programs in Asia. Economic Development and Cultural Change, 27(4), 687–704.

Geertz, C. 1963. Agricultural involution: the processes of ecological change in Indonesia. University of California Press, Berkeley, CA, USA.

Goldin, C. 1981. Family strategies and the family economy in the late nineteenth century: the role of secondary workers. In Hershberg, T., ed., Philadelphia: work, space, family and group experience in the nineteenth century: essays toward an interdisciplinary history of the city. Oxford University Press, New York, NY, USA.

Gomes, M. 1984. Family size and educational attainment in Kenya. Population and Development Review, 10(4), 647–660.

GPO (Government Printing Office). 1980. The Global 2000 Report to the President. GPO, Washington, DC, USA.

Hackenberg, R.A. 1971. The cybernetic village. Southeast Asian Journal of Sociology, 4(1), 5–27.

_____. 1980. New patterns of urbanization in Southeast Asia. Population and Development Review, 6(3), 391–419.

_____. 1982. Diffuse urbanization and the resource frontier. In Mathur, O.P., ed., Small cities and national development. United Nations Centre for Regional Development, Nagoya, Japan. pp.139–171.

_____. 1983. The urban impact of agropolital development: the changing regional metropolis in the Southern Philippines. Comparative Urban Research, 10(1), 69–98.

_____. 1984a. Farm modernization and fertility decline in the southern Philippines. Institute of Behavioral Sciences, University of Colorado, Boulder, CO, USA. Population Program Working Paper, 3.

_____. 1984b. Microurbanization: an optimizing strategy for rural and regional development. U.S. Agency for International Development, Washington, DC, USA.

Hackenberg, R.A., Magalit, H.F. 1985. Demographic responses to development: sources of declining fertility in the Philippines. Westview Press, Boulder, CO, USA.

Harkin, D.A. 1975. Strengths and weaknesses of Philippine land reform. Asia Society, New York, NY, USA. Southeast Asia Development Advisory Group Papers.

Hayami, Y., Kikuchi, M. 1978. Anatomy of a peasant economy: a rice village in the Philippines. International Rice Research Institute, Los Baños, Philippines.

_____. 1981. Asian village economy at the crossroads. Johns Hopkins University Press, Baltimore, MD, USA.

Herdt, R.W., Wickham, T.H. 1978. Exploring the gap between potential and actual rice yields. In Economic consequences of the new rice technology: Proceedings of the Conference on the Economic Consequences of New Rice Technology held at the Institute, Los Baños, 13–16 December 1976. International Rice Research Institute, Los Baños, Philippines. pp. 3–29.

Heynig, K. 1982. The principal schools of thought on the peasant economy. Comisión Económica para América Latina, Review, 16(April), 113–139.

Holmberg, A., et al. 1966. Vicos: teoría y practica de antropología aplicada. Instituto Indigebista Peruano, Lima, Peru.

IBRD (International Bank for Reconstruction and Development). 1976. The Philippines: priorities and prospects for development. World Bank, Washington, DC, USA.

_____. 1980. Aspects of poverty in the Philippines: review and assessment. World Bank, Washington, DC, USA. Report 2984-PH.

ILO (International Labor Office). 1974. Sharing in development: a program of employment, equity and growth for the Philippines. ILO, Geneva, Switzerland.

Kahn, J. 1983. Reconstituting the peasantry in Indonesia: capitalism, agrarian structure and the effectivity of concepts. Unpublished manuscript.

Kautsky, K. 1970. La cuestión agraria. Editorial Cartago, Buenos Aires, Argentina.

Kerkvliet, B. 1974. Land reform in the Philippines since the Marcos coup. Pacific Affairs, 47(3), 286–305.

Khan, A.R., Lewis, L.H. 1976. Some estimates of current levels of fertility and mortality in Bangladesh: a preliminary analysis of pregnancy histories of Bangladesh Fertility Survey Data. Paper presented at the Bangladesh Fertility Seminar, Cox's Bazaar, Bangladesh.

Khuda, B. 1977. Value of children in a Bangladesh village. In Caldwell, J.C., ed., The persistence of high fertility. Australian National University, Canberra, Australia. pp. 681–728.

_____. 1978. Labour utilization in a village economy of Bangladesh. Australian National University, Canberra, Australia. PhD thesis.

_____. 1982. Nuptiality in rural Bangladesh. Demography India, 11(1), 55–72.

_____. 1984. Population control in Bangladesh: the prospects. In Jones, G.W., ed., The demographic transition in Asia. Maruzen Asia (Pte.) Ltd, Singapore. pp. 147–169.

_____. In press. Rural development and demographic change: a case study of a Bangladesh village. University Press Ltd, Dhaka, Bangladesh.

Kikuchi, M, Hayami, H. 1983. New rice technology, intramural migration and institutional innovation in the Philippines. Population and Development Review, 9(2), 247–257.

Kocher, J.E. 1973. Rural development, income distribution and fertility decline. Population Council, New York, NY, USA.

Laderman, C. 1983. Wives and mid-wives. University of California Press, Berkeley, CA, USA.

Malaysia, Government of. 1972. Community groups. Government Printing Press, Kuala Lumpur, Malaysia.

_____. 1976a. Third Malaysian plan, 1976–80. Government Printing Press, Kuala Lumpur, Malaysia.

_____. 1976b. Selangor State Development Corporation. Government Printing Press, Kuala Lumpur, Malaysia.

_____. 1981. Fourth Malaysian plan, 1981–85. Government Printing Press, Kuala Lumpur, Malaysia.

Mamdani, M. 1973. The myth of population control: family, caste and class in an Indian village. Monthly Review Press, New York, NY, USA.

Martine, G. 1979. Adaptation of migrants or survival of the fittest. Journal of Developing Areas, 14(1), 23–41.

Martinez, H. 1969. Las migraciones altiplanicas y la colonización del Tambopata. Centro de Estudios de Población y Desarrollo, Lima, Peru.

Marx, K. 1969. El capital (Tomo 1). Fondo de Cultura Económica, Mexico City, Mexico.

Matos Mar, J., et al. 1969. Dominación y cambio en el Perú rural. Instituto de Estudios Peruanos, Lima, Peru.

Mayer, E. 1976. Reciprocidad e intercambio en los Andes Peruanos. Instituto de Estudios Peruanos, Lima, Peru.

Meillassoux, C. 1984. The economic bases of demographic reproduction: from the domestic mode of production to wage-earning. Journal of Peasant Studies, 11(1), 50–61.

Millar, J. 1970. A reformulation of Chayanov's theory of the peasant economy. Economic Development and Cultural Change, 3(9), 219–229.

Miranda, A. 1982. The demography of Bangladesh: data and issues. Christian Michelsen Institute, Bergen, Norway. Development Research and Action Program Publication 144.

Mora y Araujo, M. 1982. Teoría y datos: comentarios sobre el enfoque histórico estructural — Reflexiones téorico–metodológicos sobre investigación en población. El Colegio de México, Mexico.

Mueller, E., Anderson, J. 1982. The economic and demographic impact of the Comilla Project in Bangladesh: a case study. In Barlow, R., ed., Case studies in the demographic impact of Asian development projects. Center for Research on Economic Development, University of Michigan, Ann Arbor, MI, USA. pp. 1–54.

Nag, M. 1982. Modernization and its impact on fertility: the Indian scene. Center for Policy Studies, Population Council, New York, NY, USA. Working Paper 84.

Nun, J. 1969. Sobre población relativa, ejercito de reserva y masa marginal. Revista Latino Americana de Sociología.

Ong, A. In press. Japanese factories, Malay workers: industrialization and sexual metaphors in West Malaysia. In Errington, S., Atkinson, J., ed., The cultural construction of gender in island Southeast Asia. Cambridge University Press, Cambridge, U.K.

Peru, Government of. 1972a. Agricultural census. Lima, Peru.

_____ . 1972b. Population census. Lima, Peru.

_____ . 1981. Population census. Lima, Peru.

Perú, Ministerio de Salud. 1980. El aborto en los establecimientos de salud del Perú. Ministerio de Salud, Lima, Peru.

PSAC (President's Science Advisory Committee). 1967. The world food problem. Government Printing Office, Washington, DC, USA.

Rahim, S.A. 1971. Village cooperatives and economic development of subsistence agriculture. Bangladesh Academy for Rural Development, Comilla, Bangladesh. Mimeo.

Raper, A.F. 1970. Rural development in action: the comprehensive experiment at Comilla, East Pakistan. Cornell University Press, Ithaca, NY, USA.

Roumasset, J., Smith, J. 1981. Population, technological change and the evolution of labor markets. Population and Development Review, 7(3), 401–417.

Ruttan, V.W. 1978. New rice technology and agricultural development policy. In Economic consequences of the new rice technology: Proceedings of the Conference on the Economic Consequences of New Rice Technology held at the Institute, Los Baños, 13–16 December 1976. International Rice Research Institute, Los Baños, Philippines. pp. 367–382.

Schuman, H. 1967. Economic development and individual change. Center for International Affairs, Harvard University, Cambridge, MA, USA.

Scott, C. 1976. Peasants, proletarization and the articulation of the modes of production. Journal of Peasant Studies, 1(2), 5–28.

Scott, J.C. 1976. The moral economy of the peasant. Yale University Press, New Haven, CT, USA.

Simkins, P., Wernstedt, F. 1971. Philippine migration to the Digos-Padada Valley. Yale University Press, New Haven, CT, USA. Yale Southeast Asia Studies, Monograph 16.

Smith, B. 1979. The Comilla strategy: a systems analysis of rural development organisation. Michigan State University, East Lansing, MI, USA. PhD dissertation.

Stark, O. 1981. Research on rural-to-urban migration in LDCs: the confusion frontier and why we should pause to rethink afresh. Department of Economics, Bar-Elan University and the David Horowitz Institute for the Research of Developing Countries, Tel Aviv University, Israel. Mimeo.

Stearman, A. 1978. The highland migrant in lowland Bolivia. Human Organization, 37(2).

Stoeckel, J., Chowdhury, M.A. 1973. Infant mortality and family planning in rural Bangladesh. Oxford University Press, Dhaka, Bangladesh.

Torrado, S. 1981. Sobre los conceptos de "Estrategias familiares de vida" y "Proceso de reproducción de la fuerza de trabajo": notas téorico-metodológicas. Demografía y Economía, 15(2), 204–233.

USAID (United States Agency for International Development). 1980. Country development strategy statement, FY82. USAID Philippines, Manila, Philippines.

_____. 1981. Economic assessment of the new society and key problems facing the Republic of the Philippines. USAID Philippines, Manila, Philippines.

Vlassoff, C. 1983. Migration and fertility as 'survival strategies' — an exploratory analysis. Paper presented at the Population Association of America Annual Meeting, Pittsburgh, PA, USA, April 1983.

White, B. 1976. Production and reproduction in a Javanese village. Columbia University, New York, NY, USA. PhD thesis.

Wickham, T.H., Barker, R., Rosegrant, M.V. 1978. Complementarities among irrigation, fertilizer and modern rice varieties. In Economic consequences of the new rice technology. Proceedings of the Conference on the Economic Consequences of New Rice Technology held at the Institute, Los Baños, 13–16 December 1976. International Rice Research Institute, Los Baños, Philippines. pp. 221–232.